The Baths at Buxton Spa

Hot Baths interior c. 1935

Mike Langham & Colin Wells

CHURNET VALLEY BOOKS
1 King Street, Leek, Staffordshire. ST13 5NW 01538 399033
© Mike Langham & Colin Wells and Churnet Valley Books 2005
ISBN 1 904546 21 8

Acknowledgements

We are grateful to the people who have helped in the preparation of this book.

The staff at the Local Studies section of the Buxton Library and at the Buxton Museum and Art Gallery are now used to our many and regular enquiries which they always answer in a very helpful way. We are privileged to have access to the important Devonshire Buxton archive of papers at Chatsworth and we are most grateful to Charles Noble, the Keeper of Collections and all his staff for friendly and helpful research facilities. We thank Martin Bailey of the High Peak Borough who has explained a good deal to us about water management, Richard Tuffrey, the Borough Conservation Officer for his continuing support and the staff at the TIC. Daphne Barrett, chief executive of Infoplan International Public Relations London, has kindly updated our description of the bottled water. We are fortunate in having access to research by Ray Bradshaw on the operation of the baths in the 20th century and we thank him for the valuable contribution this has made to chapter four. It has now become an important routine for us to ask our friend, and noted local historian, Oliver Gomersal to critically appraise our work and this he has done, for the second edition, in his usual careful manner. So we have spent some time getting down to detailed editing, aided by Marjorie Gomersal who not only sustains us with tea and delicious cake but has also provided first hand descriptions of her own experiences of the baths in the 20th century. Our good friend Ian Clements has produced a number of quite exceptional original drawings and plans. We are indebted to Mr Alan W. Bednall for permission to use extracts from the diary of Mrs Cruso on her visits to Buxton in 1836.

Permission to reproduce images has been given as follows:

The Director of Sheffield Leisure Services (Sheffield Archives) for Barker's Plan, (Barker Deeds 666); Bodleian Library, University of Oxford for: 'Prospect of Buxton', (MS. Top. gen. d. 14, fol. 19r) and 'Buxton Bath July 1712', (MS. Top. gen. e. 61, fol. 14r); The John Carr plans by courtesy of the trustees of Sir John Soane's Museum, London; The Bath Archaeological Trust have kindly loaned the image of the Roman bath at Bath; thanks to EM & GJ Barton for two images; The 1803/6 White plan (map 2042) and F. Langley's 1915 plan of the Natural Baths are from the Devonshire Collection reproduced by permission of the Chatsworth Settlement Trustees; the Roman milestone and portrait of Charles Cotton from the Journals of the Derbyshire Archaeological Society; Buxton Museum and Art Gallery for several images from their extensive and historically valuable collection; Robert Hale Ltd for 'The Georgian Scene' from *Buxton under the Dukes of Devonshire* by R. Grundy Heape, 1948; two illustrations are from *Memoir of Thomas Bewick* published by John Lane, The Bodley Head. We thank them all. Other illustrations are from the authors' collections.

An Enviable Invalid

PROLOGUE

Bathing - the immersion of our bodies in water - has a history which traces as far back as the very existence of the human species on this planet. According to the Hellenic saga, Jupiter with a thunderbolt created a live spring for the thirsty Hercules and throughout Greece, thermal springs were dedicated to Hercules. Many springs were considered sacred in antiquity, even though they contained ordinary water, if such springs were marked by some unusual characteristic, for example: if they did not go dry, or freeze in winter, or if they welled up through vapour or carbonic acid or possessed a disagreeable taste, they were held to be salutary for those in health and health-bringing for the sick. Among the Greeks, Æsculapius, the healing god, was naturally connected with baths and springs, which through him gained curative properties, even though they contained ordinary water. According to Aristides, the wells of Æsculapius at Pergamon even restored speech to the dumb; it was said that those partaking of the water could prophesy.[1]

Bathing through time has been seen to have a threefold purpose, for cleansing, for medicine, and for pleasure; sometimes the major reason for bathing has been for one of these, at other times for more than one, perhaps all three. The Romans, for example, were great bathers who devised sophisticated series of bath houses, typically consisting of three stages, Frigidarium or cold bath, Tepidarium or tepid bath and a hot bath, Calidarium together with hot air and steam baths. Elaborate arrangements involving under-floor heating or hypocaust were used to heat the water in their baths and rooms to the required temperatures. We know too that the Romans had a sophisticated social structure and the baths were often used as places to conduct business and for social gatherings. During the occupation of Britain the Romans constructed forts and settlements, many of which were equipped with bathing facilities. There is good evidence to suggest that they built a complex of baths in Buxton as will be seen in this book.

After the departure of the Romans from Britain a period of several hundred years passed by, which we now commonly refer to as the Dark Ages due to the scarcity of written material available from these times. But archaeological investigations indicate that the practice of bathing became less frequent, possibly due to the lack of an efficient distribution and storage system for the water. Use would undoubtedly have been made of the naturally occurring facilities provided by mother nature in the form of springs and it is no accident that the warm springs of Bath in Somerset and Buxton, high in the Derbyshire hills, have been celebrated through time.

In Mediaeval times resorting to a holy well or mineral spring to seek a cure for particular ailments became an accepted medical remedy and doctors began to offer specialist advice. Dr John Jones (1572) who wrote on Buxton and Bath, and Dr Robert Lessee, who wrote a treatise on the waters at Bath in Somerset (c.1580), set out regimes for bathing and drinking the water together with appropriate prayers to be said at the bath side. The 'cure' was in part medical and in part belief in God, but the spa also provided a venue to meet others, socialise and engage in leisure activity. This habit of visiting the baths, though often involving difficult and tiring journeys, became an accepted part of the social routine of the nobility, with humbler people drawn in their wake. In this way, the secular holiday began to emerge.[2]

The term spa or spaw was developed in use by Sir William Paddy and Dr Richard Andrews who visited the resort of Spa, in Belgium in the early 17th century. They promoted the term for use in England in places where there were springs of a similar chemical composition to the Spa waters. In time the term became generic and was applied to '...all resorts where people went both to drink the waters and to bathe in them...'[3] This definition encompasses both inland and seaside resorts including those resorts at the seaside which offered sea-water bathing, such as New Brighton, and those which combined such bathing with the use of mineral springs, such as Scarborough.[4] Dr Thomas Short, in his seminal work on mineral waters published in 1734, describes 104 spas or spaws in 95 different locations in the counties of Derbyshire, Lincolnshire and Yorkshire alone.[5] Many of these, however, were small insignificant springs which would not measure up to the definition of a spa as described above, and there were many such springs throughout the country used simply to obtain a good, clean water.

In reality, to be seen as a proper spa a place should also have had its water described and approved by a medical practitioner. So, for example, the 'sulphurous or chalybeate spring' used by householders in Ilkeston, near Nottingham in the 19th century, would not qualify as a spa.[6] Birley Spa near Sheffield, developed from 1843 by Earl Manvers, offered a large plunging bath and a chalybeate spring (iron bearing water) together with a bath hotel and might come within the definition were it possible to associate a medical man with this centre.[7] Weymouth, on the other hand, though developed by local businessman Thomas Shore in the 1830s, had the imprimatur of Dr Robert Graves in 1792 and, at the request of Shore, received analysis and confirmation of its efficacy by a professor at Guys Hospital.[8] It therefore meets the definition.

The Victorian era saw the greatest expansion in bathing innovation. Straight bathing in deep or shallow pools had always been available but the water application techniques developed markedly during this period. It was sprayed in all directions - from above, from beneath and horizontally, and all three at once. Heated to boiling point and turned into vapour, the water was inhaled in vapour and used in Turkish baths. The introduction of 'hydropathy' from the 1830s placed the emphasis upon the medico-water regime rather than the inherent properties of the water itself. Thus ordinary water could be used in a plethora of different ways, sheets were soaked with it and were wrapped around the body; mixed with mud and peat it was used to fill shallow baths in which to bathe the body; frozen into blocks the stuff was applied to the naked abdomen for the treatment of liver disorders. In later years the addition of electricity to the bath brought in an extra dimension to the experience and an element of danger which had the capability of exciting the patient in more ways than one! Taken internally the water was advised as beneficial for most, if not all complaints of the digestive system. Taken rectally the water was considered to be of benefit to colonic disorders. At the turn of the century the science of Balneology and Climatology could offer a huge range of treatments using water, air, electricity, radiation, lubrication, dry heat and many medicated forms of bath. From this emerged the recognised specialisms of physio and hydro-therapy.

With hindsight it may seem odd to us that the water cure was undertaken to such an extent. Even at its height water bathing, hydropathy, hydrotherapy and balneology elicited some degree of scepticism. But at a time when the developing pharmacopoeia included drugs such as morphine, colchicum, quinine, acetate of lead, sulphur and tobacco and when the doctor's income was dependent upon the sale of these drugs, it is perhaps not surprising that people would often choose a, by-and-large, less risky course of treatment. The operative word here is 'cure' for undoubtedly relief was to be found from bathing and hydrotherapy by those suffering rheumatic disease, even if this did not lead to a permanent cure. Today, in addition to hydrotherapy, a range of prescription drugs seek to bring about similar relief from the almost 200 different forms of rheumatic disease, a condition which is still difficult to manage clinically and for which there is still no permanent cure.

The story of spas and springs and water medicine is one of changing social mores and fashions. Today drinking bottled spring water is increasingly popular and there is renewed interest in some of the spa treatments of the past. Unlike in Britain, many countries in the rest of Europe have continued to support spa centres to the present day and it is European commercial expertise which is influencing the resurgence of spa health in Britain. Buxton in the High Peak, with an illustrious history as an inland resort is, once again, reinventing itself to exploit its natural mineral water and its long-rooted expertise in spa management. Buxton Water is a commercially successful bottled water throughout the world; the University of Derby has established a School of Hospitality and Tourism which will offer degree and other qualification courses in Health Beauty and Spa Management; the famous Crescent will be developed and is set to rival Bath with a spa hotel, shops, a re-furbished Assembly Rooms, an Interpretation Centre, and a Spa Health facility. Buxton is poised to become Buxton Spa once again.

This book is a major revision of our *History of the Baths at Buxton*, first published in 1997 and for a while out of print. We have taken the opportunity to add a great deal of new material on the social history of the spa collected during our on-going research over the last seven years. This is augmented by anecdotal quotes and writings of visitors through time, and an updated glossary of the many forms of water treatment or 'balneology' offered in the Buxton Spa. It provides a companion book to our *History of the Devonshire Royal Hospital at Buxton* published in 2003

ML & CW September 2004

'...Hither the Sick, the Lame, and Barren come, And hence go healthful, Sound and fruitful home. Buxton's in Beauty famous; but in this Much more, the Pilgrim never frustrate is, That comes to bright St. Anne...'

Charles Cotton 'The Wonders of the Peake' 1681

...The custom of attending on watering places, as they are called, is often attributed to fashion, and has been exposed in severe terms, as an improper desertion of business and family affairs. In some instances this may be the case, and in such it deserves to be reprobated in the strongest language. In general, however, many and great allowances are to be made for these excursions..'

Dr. Jos. Denman MD. 1801.

'...Buxton - The Mountain Spa! the name, to anyone familiar with the town, is suggestive of stately buildings, pleasant gardens, well-kept walks and drives, clean streets, high hills, baths and bath-chairs, mineral waters, the arrival and departure of valetudinarians, good music and, given a reasonable amount of fine weather, a feeling of satisfaction with things in general, and with the health-imparting qualities of the place in particular! For Buxton is, and has ever been, a health resort "par excellence"...'

The "Borough Guide" to Buxton, Ed. J. Burrow, Cheltenham, c.1910

'...The scheme proposes to open the UK's first true spa hotel for over 100 years. The hotel will be linked to a state of the art natural thermal spa in the Natural Baths. Alongside this, a new visitor centre is proposed to enable the public to learn about the story of Buxton's spa heritage and see some of the magnificent Georgian interiors. Finally, the public will, once again, be able to "take the waters" in the elegant surroundings of the town's Victorian Pump Room...'

'The Buxton Crescent & Spa Project', briefing paper,
High Peak Borough and Derbyshire County Councils, 2004.

'...I feel fortunate in sharing the responsibility with CP Holdings/Danubius Hotels of healing the scars to Buxton's heart, quickening its pulse by the re-creation of the thermal spa without which this masterpiece of architecture, Buxton Crescent, could not have been created....'

Trevor Osborne, Chairman The Osborne Group,
from Crescent Times Issue 1 Autumn 2004.

CONTENTS

Cover of Buxton Guide
Book 1914

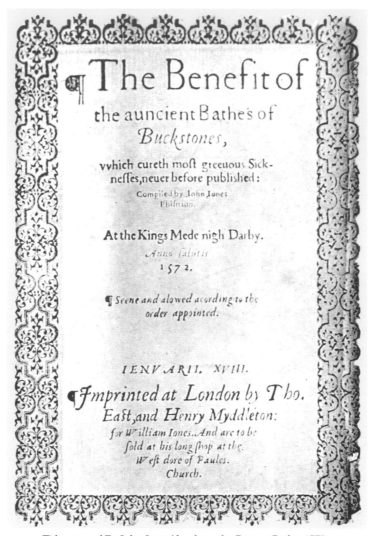

¶ The Benefit of
the auncient Bathes of
Buckstones,

vvhich cureth moſt greeuous Sick-
neſſes, neuer before publiſhed:

Compiled by John Jones
Phiſition.

At the Kings Mede nigh Darby.

Anno ſalutis
1572.

¶ Seene and alowed according to the
order appointed.

IENVARII. XVIII.

¶ Imprinted at London by Tho.
Eaſt, and Henry Myddleton:
for William Iones. And are to be
ſold at his long ſhop at the.
Weſt dore of Paules.
Church.

Title page of Dr John Jones' book on the Buxton Baths, 1572.

Appendix 1:

Temperature Conversion

In the text we have used the Fahrenheit (F) measurement which was most frequently used in this country until decimalisation. The conversion formulæ are: Fahrenheit to Celsius = (F - 32) x 0.55   Celsius to Fahrenheit = (1.8 x C) + 32

Currency

Imperial currency used pounds (£), shillings (s) and pence (d) where £1 = 20s. and 1s. = 12d.

Upon conversion in 1971 the convention became pounds (£) and pence (p) where £1 = 100p.

Approximate conversions for some currency found in the book are: 8d. = 3p; 1s.= 5p; 2s. = 10p; 2s.6d. = 12p; 3s. 4d. = 17p; 4s. = 20p; 5s. = 25p; 6s. = 30p; 6s.8d. = 34p; 7s.6d. = 37p; 10s. = 50p; 13s. 4d. = 67p; 30s. = £1.50p; £2.12s.6d. = £2.62p; £3.10s. = £3.50p; 40s. = £2. One guinea was 21s. or £1.05p; 4 guineas (£4.4s.) = £4.20p; 5 guineas (£5.5s.) = £5.25p; 10 guineas (£10.10s.) = £10.50p; 20 guineas = £21.

Measurement

Imperial measurement uses yards (yds.) feet (ft.) and inches where 12 inches = 1ft. and 3ft. = 1 yd. The decimal system uses metres (m), centimetres (cm) and millimetres (mm) where 1m = 100cm and 1cm = 100mm. Common conversions are: 25mm = 1 inch; 2.5cm = 1inch; 300mm. = 1ft; 1m. = 3ft. 3inches or 39 inches.

Official analysis of Buxton's mineral water in 2004 By permission of Buxton Mineral Water Company Ltd.

	mg/l		
Calcium	55	Magnesium	19
Sodium	24	Potassium	1
Bicarbonates	248	Chloride	37
Sulphates	13	Nitrates	<0.1
Iron	0	Aluminium	0
Total dissolved solids at 180°C	280	PH at source 7.4	

INTRODUCTORY NOTES

The Water and its Origins

Buxton Spa has become famous through the years for its natural thermal water and it is difficult to imagine how the town would have developed without this unique natural resource. Only one other British watering place, Bath, can boast a natural thermal water although the water there emerges from the ground at a considerably higher temperature than Buxton's. The definition of Thermal Water by the Institute of Geological Sciences, is *'...those waters, which at their point of emergence have the same or a greater temperature than the mean average for the surrounding air...'*

Buxton water emerges from several springs, covering an area of roughly one acre, at a constant temperature of 82°F (27.5°C). The origin of the water has been a subject of conjecture throughout history but modern consensus favours the theory that rainfall to the east of the town sinks down through the limestone layers to a great depth and rises again to the surface under hydrostatic pressure. It is deduced that a fault line exists in the limestone running north-north-east, continuing over the site of the springs and providing a water route to the surface. Measurements of the tritium content indicate that the water has been underground for many, possibly thousands, of years. The unusually high temperature of the water can be attributed to it rising from a great depth where it is geothermally heated by the earth's interior. With the water rise bubbles of gas, mostly nitrogen and carbon dioxide. Analyses of the water have been conducted over the years with varying levels of accuracy but the main constituent is calcium and this is not surprising given the terrain. A present day analysis appears in Appendix 1.

Chalybeate Water

In addition to the thermal water, the town has at least one chalybeate (pronounced kal-i-be-at) spring which emerges from a narrow band of shale lying between the limestone and gritstone formations on the north side of the Crescent. Chalybeate or ferruginous water contains iron and was used as a general tonic for anaemic conditions and as an eye bath. It was exploited up until the middle part of the 20th century but today sites of the springs are not easy to locate and the water is no longer available to us.

Orientation

The Crescent in Buxton faces south east but, for reasons of clarity in describing the positions of buildings in its locality, we have used the assumption that it faces south. This should help in interpreting the direct quotes of some of the early writers who assumed that the Crescent faced south.

Location of Principal Baths

The principal baths in the Crescent have been described over the years by historians who have used various names. To avoid confusion we have adopted the convention of calling the original Baths at the west end of the Crescent the Natural Baths and those at the east end of the Crescent the Hot Baths.

St Anne

As no standard exists for the spelling of the Buxton saint, the earlier form Anne has been adopted throughout in preference to Ann except where the name appears in a direct quotation.

Treatments Described

Throughout this book reference is made to particular forms of treatment undertaken by those visiting the Baths. In appendix 2 there is a glossary describing the many kinds of treatments available at Buxton.

Temperature Measurement

Since this is a history we have adopted the convention of quoting temperatures in degrees Fahrenheit with the more modern Celsius measurement in brackets thus: 63.8°F (17.7°C). The equations we have used for conversion are given in appendix 1.

Examples of the Buxton votive coin find 1975.

Remains of the Bath House at Chester's Roman Fort on Hadrian's Wall, Northumberland.

CHAPTER ONE

Earliest Users of the Water

Archaeological excavations in the 1980s have shown that the earliest settlement known in Buxton dates to the late Mesolithic (Middle Stone Age) period about 5300 BC. These excavations, on Lismore fields, also showed occupation sometime during the Neolithic, or New Stone Age, period (3500-1800 BC).[1] Other archaeological research has identified Neolithic burial tombs and henge monuments near Buxton, and stone circles and barrows associating Buxton with settlements through the Beaker and Bronze Ages to the Iron Age people known as the Celts.[2] The Buxton historian Arthur Jewitt, writing in 1811, paints a colourful picture of the possible origins of a settlement at Buxton. Of the Ancient Britons he says:

'...The Britons...worshipped the stars of heaven under various appelations, and had also their deities adapted to particular occasions. The Druids were their priests, their legislators, their physicians, their philosophers. To them were known the virtues of every plant, the nature of every fossil, and the properties of every spring...'

He suggests that, from the existence of burial mounds, Buxton was well known to the Druids, and goes on to say:

'...from the general knowledge they are purported to have possessed, we may be warranted in concluding that they were no strangers to the sanative powers of the springs to which Buxton owes its present celebrity. Buxton, like Bath, in all probability owed its origin to its waters alone. Its warm springs might be recommended by the Druids as a gentle alternative in some prevalent disorder; the invalids whilst waiting the slow effects of the waters, might erect a few temporary huts around their sources, and these being tenanted in succession might soon become permanent dwellings, and thus lay the foundation of a village which, at the present day, stands almost unrivalled in England...' [3]

Jewitt's conjecture is supported by place-name evidence. The Roman name for Buxton was Aquae Arnemetiae, the term 'aquae', meaning mineral springs or waters, was used to describe only one other settlement, that of Bath in Somerset (Aquae Sulis). The second part of the name may be a derivation of the Celtic word 'nemeton' or 'sacred grove' and this would suggest a religious centre at Buxton of some importance to generations of native Britons before the Roman occupation. Derivations of the name appear on altars from Brough as Arnomecte and Bath as Nemetona. The Romans tolerated and actually incorporated local cults into their beliefs and Buxton's Roman name means the mineral springs of the Goddess of the sacred grove, Arnemetia, a Celtic deity.[4]

Roman Remains

The earliest firm evidence of the existence of a bath using the thermal waters occurs in Roman times and it is likely that Buxton was a Romano-British settlement of some significance. The town stands on the intersection of a number of important Roman roads, the evidence for roads connecting Buxton (Aquae Arnemetiae) with forts at Derby (Little Chester); Brough (Anavio); Manchester (Mamucium); Melandra (Ardotalia) and possibly Chesterton, near Newcastle-under-Lyme, via Leek, has been set out by Wroe.[5] Roman finds on the Silverlands include a Roman milestone discovered in 1856 (but not

Right (proper).   Full front.   Left (proper).
Roman Mile-stone found at Buxton.

Three views of the Roman milestone found at Buxton

reported until 1862) which was dug up near a gateway leading to the later London & North Western Railway goods station in Higher Buxton. The inscription, according to Tristram, translates as:

> '....*Invested with the power of a Tribune - Consul for the second time*
> *- Father of his Country - To Anavio twelve thousand paces*',

which is twelve Roman miles.[6] During the construction of Holker Road, in about 1898, Roman finds included bronze axes and an earthenware vessel, and later finds on Silverlands have included Samian ware pottery, Roman glass and fragments of bronze, iron and lead. It has been concluded from these and other finds, including the presence of hearths and remains of querns, that there was a Romano-British settlement on the Silverlands. A comparison of the quality of pottery found on Silverlands with that discovered by Micah Salt at a cave in Deep Dale, about 3 miles from Buxton, has led to the further suggestion that Roman people of some wealth occupied Buxton, since the Deep Dale cave appears to have been used by those who had fled from Buxton when under attack.[7]

There is good recent evidence of a Romano-British settlement at Staden, just south of the town, which consisted of a collection of homesteads with enclosures forming courtyards, and a cultivated field system. The evidence suggests mixed farming generating enough wealth for the occupants to enjoy luxuries such as wine and jewellery and the likelihood that this settlement supplied the spa at Buxton.[8] Other recent evidence has emerged from excavations at Poole's Cavern, the show cave in Buxton, where extensive finds suggest Roman occupation from the first to the third centuries AD. Most importantly, the large numbers of brooches and the wide variety of pottery found offer evidence for one of the few sites in Britain of Roman jewellery manufacture and a bronze smithy.[9]

Given this evidence for a settlement and the Roman practice of defence through a series of forts connected by well made roads, it has been assumed that Buxton would have had a fort. Such a structure would have been made of earth with turf ramparts and wooden palisades and towers such as those built at Brough and Melandra by AD 78. Later forts would have been of stone.[10] Three possible sites have been put forward, one by Edward Tristram in 1916 who argued for a fort sited at the top of Bath Road.[11] His argument, based mainly on the elevation and defensive position of the site and the possible junction of Roman roads, is not strong, however, and we know of no further fieldwork on his theory. More generally it has been felt that the fort site is most likely to have been on the naturally defensive plateau of Silverlands and this has been the area of a good deal of excavation, some of which we have already described. More recent evidence, which includes aerial photography, has proved negative and a review by the Trent & Peak Archaeological Trust, which includes their own excavation work on the site of the former Girls School, has led to the conclusion that no Roman fort existed in the Silverlands area.[12] The third suggested site is the Market Place which has yielded some Roman finds; it offers a large undisturbed area. Senior's map of 1631 shows it as a large rectangular open space, and the possible junction of roads lends some support, but, in the absence of firmer evidence, it must remain in the realms of speculation.

The fort has so far proved elusive but there is evidence for a substantial and wealthy settlement which supports the case for a Roman spa, a centre for rest and recuperation probably for both military and civilian population. Given this proposition we should look carefully at the evidence for a Roman bathing complex.

Roman Baths

Remains of a Roman bath were reported by Dr Charles Leigh writing in 1700 after one of his visits to Buxton, when he described

> '...a Roman Wall cemented with red Roman Plaister, close by St Ann's Well, where we may see the Ruines of the ancient Bath, its Dimensions and Length. This Plaister is red and hard as Brick, a Mixture not prepared in these Days...'[13]

The difficulty we have with this description is that Leigh does not make clear whether the 'Roman Plaistered Wall' is the same as the 'Ruines of the ancient Bath'. It seems likely, however, that the wall is the remains of a Roman structure surrounding St Anne's Well as the physician Thomas Short, writing in 1734, says that:

> '...St Anne's well formerly rose up into a stone basin shut up within an ancient Roman brick wall, a yard square within and a yard high on three sides till Sir Thomas Delves built the present Arch over it...', and his further description confirms the position of St Anne's Well '...twenty four yards north of the outer bath...'[14]

John Speed's map of 1610 carries an engraving of St Anne's Well which could fit Short's description and position. Recent analysis by a local historian suggests that the original St Anne's Well was located under the third pier of the western end of the present Crescent.[15]

Thomas Short also describes the remains of a further bath,

> '...About thirty six years ago, when Mr White, then of Buxton-Hall, was driving up a Level to the Bath, fifty Yards East of St Anne's Well, and fourteen Yards North of Bingham Spring, the Workmen found buried deep under the Grass and Corn-mould, Sheets of Lead spread upon Great Beams of Timber, about four Yards Square, with broken Ledges round about, which had been a Leaden Cystern, and not unlikely, that of the Romans, or some other antient Bath which

had been supplied with Water from the Bingham Well...'

He is referring, here, to the discovery made by Cornelius White, proprietor of the Hall (the present day Old Hall Hotel) who made a number of improvements to the Hall and Baths in 1695/6. However, Sir John Floyer MD writing in 1697 offers a more contemporaneous account of White's improvements which differs from Short in a number of important ways,

'...New Improvements at Buxton Baths AD 1695 and 1696 by Cornelius White... By taking off some of the cold Springs from the hot, the antient Bath repaired and paved, and a new one made for the better conveniency of the poor and impotent; And a sough about 200 yards in length to drain both, for the cleaning thereof every day... About the middle of the Sough a Cistern of lead was found two yards square, and one foot deep, being four yards within the earth, supported by several oaken planks: Something higher in the same Sough, was found a place seven Yards wide, and twenty Yards long, being smooth and even on both sides and at the bottom, two Yards deep in the Earth and made of Stone...'[16]

Floyer's account is important on three counts. Firstly he mentioned improvements to the ancient bath which we take to be the one adjacent to the Hall. Secondly he described the lead bath or cistern as six feet square by one foot deep buried 12 feet under the ground. This is half the size of that described by Short. Thirdly he described a much larger structure which might be a bath but could be foundations for something else since he described it as a 'place' and gave insufficient measurements for a bath, but indicated that it was buried six feet under the ground.

Another discovery was made in 1781 during the building of the Crescent when a new tepid spring was identified close to the remains of a rectangular bath 15 by 30 feet. The floor of the bath was of red plaster 6 inches thick with a boat shaped cavity at one end, the water entered at the west end through a wide lead pipe and exited at the east end through a floodgate. The bath wall was 3 foot high and constructed of limestone covered with a strong cement, strong oak beams were laid on the top of the walls firmly connected together at the corners. The location of this bath was 6 yards from the Bath Room which, in 1781, was the room housing the main inner bath adjacent to the Hall. The medical doctor, Jos. Denman, writing in 1793, gave a similar description but was sceptical of the extent of Roman finds inferring that contemporary writers had tended to embroider the facts a little. Paradoxically, he gave the recollections of two men who worked on the building of the Crescent which add more to the original description. They confirm the size and shape of the bath but add that 10 feet from the bath on the north side was what they thought to be a drinking well built of gritstone which had a flight of steps more than 7 feet deep.[17] Pearson, writing in 1784, used the findings of a Mr Watson in 1780 who described two baths, in the larger one with the plaster floor, he said there were some bottles, supposedly Roman; the second bath was smaller and had a wall of stone.[18]

A further and most important find was made in August 1975 during reconstruction work on the floor of the 20th century swimming pool, situated over hot and cold springs in the Natural baths, when a brick structure was unearthed together with 232 Roman coins, 3 bronze bracelets and a wire clasp. Subsequent research suggests that these were offerings to the Celtic goddess Arnemetia and the dates of the coins, which range largely from 100 AD to 400 AD, indicate these offerings were made throughout the period of Roman occupation. Close by the Roman deposit, jewellery spanning the 16th to 18th centuries was found together with a number of 17th century pins which were also used as offerings.[19]

A Roman Spa Complex

The difficulty in analysing this evidence is that the early writers differ in their descriptions of size and location of remains. Great care is needed in determining the orientation of directions given and more detailed work is needed to site the bath remains with any degree of precision.

Nevertheless, it is possible to suggest that there were, broadly, three areas over the spring sources forming the sites of Roman baths. These are shown in the illustration as:

(A) the Natural Baths area where the votive coin find and the references in early writings to an 'ancient bath' suggest Roman use;

(B) the western wing of the Crescent where we have the remains found in 1781 and the St Anne's Well observations of 1700 and more recently;

(C) east of the centre of the Crescent where the lead bath remains were unearthed in 1697.

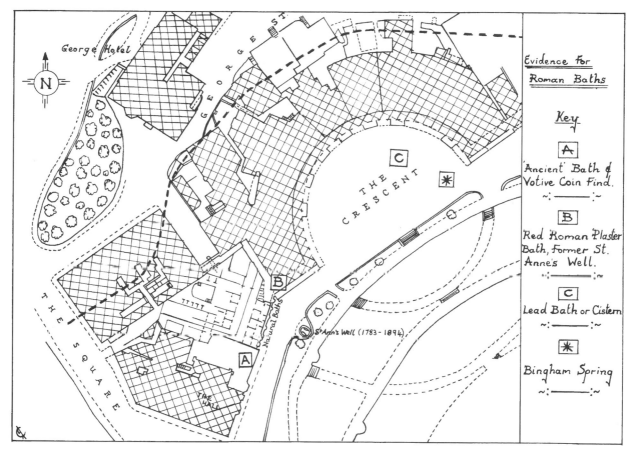

Evidence for Roman baths

Given this evidence what, typically, might a Roman bath complex at Aquae Arnemetiae have looked like? The most usual provision in public baths was a route involving three types of bath, tepid [Tepidarium], hot [Calidarium] and cold [Frigidarium]. These would be built into a complex which included changing rooms with niches for clothes, a latrine and a furnace for heating the water. The warm, wet atmosphere created by the baths gave rise to high levels of building maintenance and, for this reason, the roofs of bath houses were often barrel-vaulted. Chesters Roman fort on Hadrian's Wall has good remains of a bath complex situated between the fort and the river Tyne from which it is fed by aqueduct. A plan of the site shows an arrangement of hot and cold baths, and hot dry and steam rooms. A reconstruction shows barrel vaulted roofs over the hot steam rooms and bath and the warm rooms. Traces of pink mortar from the lower walls of the hot baths are still visible. Nearer to Buxton the remains of a bath house have been identified at Melandra near Glossop.[20]

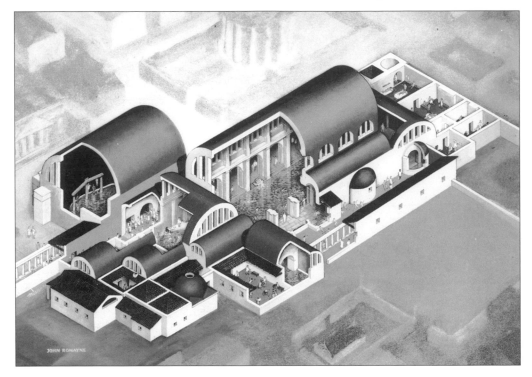

Reconstruction of the Roman baths at Bath

Buxton (Aquae Arnemetiae) shares the name 'aquae' meaning waters or mineral springs with Bath in Somerset (Aquae Sulis) and it is interesting to speculate whether Buxton might have had a modest version of the temple and baths complex at Bath. A reconstruction of Roman Bath shows the sacred spring covered with a barrel-vaulted roof forming a focal point of a religious complex, with the classical temple of Sulis-Minerva alongside, the two buildings being set inside a walled precinct. Adjacent to the spring, but outside the precinct, was a complex of baths some with barrel-vaulted roofs. Distribution of the water from the spring source to the baths involved the use of lead pipes and reservoirs built of stone on timber piles and lead-lined. The Great Bath was also lead-lined.

Buxton has the remains of such bath materials and the votive coin find offers evidence of worship to at least one deity, the Goddess Arnemetia. There is other evidence of a possible shrine on the Slopes or St Anne's Cliff, referred to as 'Staincliffe' by Major Rooke in his archaeological work of 1787-88. He excavated an 'oblong tumulus' discovering an unmortared wall 22½ feet by 46 feet having an upper-structure of dressed stone. He found also tiles, nails and a Roman potsherd. Major Rooke thought this to be a Roman temple but modern interpretations differ over whether this was a shrine and the actual evidence is limited. [21]

The possibilities are there but much archaeological work would be required around the spring sources and the Slopes to begin to verify the scenario we have suggested. But, taking all the available evidence set out in this chapter, it is entirely reasonable to propose that extensive commercial exploitation of the natural warm and cold springs took place in Roman Buxton.

Anglo Saxon and Danish

The Romans withdrew their government of Britain in about 410 AD leaving the native Romano-Britons to face invasion by the Angles, Saxons and Jutes of Northern Germany and Denmark who settled initially in the more fertile south and east. Movement into the Peak District took place via the rivers Trent, Derwent and Dove in the late 6th century and the rivers Mersey, Etherow and Goyt in the 7th century. The many small tribes which made up the invasions gradually formed into seven separate kingdoms. One of these, Mercia (meaning 'borderland'), extended over the greater part of the midlands and included North Derbyshire. A surviving document called the Tribal Hidage, drawn up in mid to late 7th century, probably to assess the taxable value of Mercia, tells us that the settlers in North Derbyshire were known as Pecsaetan or 'Peak-dwellers'.

The northern border of Mercia was with the Northumbrians, led by King Eadwine (Edwin) who brought Christianity to Northumbria, through the priest Paulinus, and built a church at York. The first recorded Christian missionary in Mercia was Paulinus who preached and baptised at Littleborough (Notts) in 627. The existence of place names in the Peak District such as Eccles Cross and Eccles Pike, suggest sites of early British Christianity. The name 'Eccles' derives from the Celtic ecclesia meaning church and suggests there was a Christian congregation here by the early part of the 6th century. This would not necessarily be a church in terms of a building but communal meetings would have been held often near a stone cross. Eccles Pike offered a recognisable landmark for the evangelist. But the invading Anglo Saxons were pagan, thus when Christianity reached the Peak dwellers in the mid 7th century it was, in some part, a reintroduction.

The Roman road from the river Trent to Buxton guided the early Anglian settlers on their way north, the concentration of barrow burials along this road, past the Prehistoric henge monument Arbor Low, and including the very important finds at Benty Grange, confirm this. The Roman road to Brough was known, in the 16th century, as Bath Gate and later as Batham Gate, but the oldest recorded form of the name is 'Bathomgate' which is pure Old English and provides strong evidence for Buxton being a bathing place in Anglo-Saxon times.[22] A vicarious glimpse of how the bath might have looked is given in a piece of Anglo Saxon poetry called 'The Ruin' which is thought to be describing the hot springs at Bath in Somerset: '...*Well wrought this wall: Fate broke it. Bright were the buildings, Halls where springs ran... stood stone houses: wide streams welled hot from source and a wall all caught in its bright bosom...*'[23]

Mercia was annexed by the invading Vikings in 874, who founded the new borough of Derby, and Buxton was presumably accessible via the Roman road. The reconquest of the area in about 920, by Edward the Elder, resulted in the building of a fort in Bakewell and by 966, when Edgar had united the two kingdoms of Britain north and south of the river Thames to become the 'king of the whole of Britain', the area incorporating Bakewell, Ashford and Hope was a single region of some wealth. During this period of nearly 700 years we can only speculate that the warm springs of Buxton would have been been used for bathing, if not for curative purposes. Whilst there is no firm archaeological or written evidence for this, the later use of the springs suggests a continuing, if tenuous, line of use.

Mediaeval Springs and Shrine

There is no mention of Buxton in the Domesday survey of 1086, though Wormhill [Wruenele] and Tideswell [Tideswelle] are both included. However, since the survey can be seen as an administrative exercise designed to inform King William of the wealth of his kingdom, it set out to identify estates which could produce a taxable income. The last question asked by his commissioners is telling, '...*Can more be got?...*'[24]

Buxton at the beginning of the 12th century was primarily a cattle pasturing place and may have been so at the time of the Domesday survey. Archaeological and place name evidence for Staden, just outside Buxton, suggests a mediaeval settlement dating from the early 12th century including a longhouse.[25] At this time William Peveril gave land to found Lenton Abbey in Nottinghamshire and the foundation charter dated between 1100-08 gives the origin of Buxton as Buc(k)stanes, though the variation Buchestanes was also known from 1108. The name may derive from bucc and stan meaning buck stones (as in deer) or, more likely, Bug-stan meaning rocking stones.[26]

There are a number of variations on the name, for example the term Kyngesbucstones was known by 1366 and suggests that Buxton was associated with the Forest of the Peak. King Richard II was evidently in the neighbourhood of Buxton between September 1399 and February 1400 prior to his death in Yorkshire. It is possible that St Anne's Well was named after his queen, Anne of Bohemia, whom he married in 1382. Up to that time the name had been uncommon in England but in that same year, Anne, the apocryphal mother of the Virgin Mary, who was a cult figure associated with miracles of healing, was recognised as a saint and the observance of her feast made obligatory throughout England, by Pope Urban VI in response to a petition. Law suits presented in Chancery in the early 16th century speak of the well chapel having existed '...*out of time of mind of man...*' and '...*all times whereof no memory of man extended to the contrary...*' suggesting that the chapel at the well had been in use for a very long time going back, perhaps, at least 150 years to the time of King Richard II.[27] An alternative, but less plausible, account for the name 'St Anne' concerns the discovery of a statue of a Goddess by the Cotterell family who came into possession of the land on which the chapel and well stood in 1489. It is suggested that the statue was of the Roman Goddess Arnemetia and the first four letters inscribed on it were misread as Anne. Dr John Jones writing in 1572 was sceptical, however, and he wrote; '...*and as for Cotterell's tale, or the vayne invencions about S. Anne found in the well, or of the water set from flood Jordan, I reckon them not worthy the recital. Therefore I will not detayne you with such tryfles...*'[28]

This may have been a tale, then, put out by the Cotterell's to drum up business, though we know there was an image of St Anne removed from the well chapel in 1538.

The earliest written evidence we have for a well at Buxton occurs about 1460 when William Worcester, also known as Botoner, wrote an 'itinerarium' of places he had probably visited during his lifetime. He describes Buxton as follows:

'...*Memorandum that Halywell, the source of the waters of Wye, in the county of Derby, about 100 miles from London, makes many miracles making the infirm healthy, and in winter it is warm, even as honeyed milk...*'[29]

He incorrectly attributes the source of the river Wye to the mineral springs but his description indicates that the well was in use at this time for medicinal purposes and the 'cures' were associated with both the warmth of the water and religious belief. Further confirmation is given in the 'inquisition post mortem' of John Talbot, second Earl of Shrewsbury who was killed in the battle of Northampton in 1460. He owned the Manor of Chelmorton, twenty acres of land at Fairfield and *'one rood of land at Bukston juxta Halywell'*. Access to Buxton would not have been easy at that time, though we know from a legal case of 1490 that there was a road from Ashbourne to Buxton called 'Alsope Way'.[30] From a will of 1493-4, we learn of 'Buxtonford Chapel', the earliest written mention of a chapel, the entry also suggesting that the river Wye had a ford rather than a bridge.

The detailed household accounts kept by the steward of Sir Henry Willoughby (an ancestor of Lord Middleton) between 1521-26 suggest visits by the gentry at Buxton:

'......Item Tuesday the 27 of June for your reward to two women that
washed lead ore as ye went to Saint Anne's 2d.
Item for my Master's costs at Saint Anne's of Bucstone, the 7th day of September, 7s. 6d.
Item for my Master's offering to Saint Anne's sent by Clyfton, 4d.....' [31]

From this time there is much evidence for the continuing use of the waters. In 1569 a play written by John Heywood, a Londoner, included St Anne of Buxton as one of a number of sacred shrines, and the famous and perhaps earliest English antiquary, John Leland who travelled between 1533 and 1539, included *'S. Anne of Bukstanes Welle'* in his account. In 1535 Henry VIII instituted a national enquiry to determine the value of the church's wealth, prior to the dissolution of the monasteries, but no information could be obtained about the value of offerings at the shrine. However, in about the same year the jewels, goods and chattels at the Well were the subject of a legal dispute between the executors of the Vicar of Bakewell and the Chaplain of Buxton, Thomas Turner, in which their value was given as forty marks [£26] and it may be because of this that the value of the offerings was kept from the commissioners.

The Well and chapel did not escape the attention of Thomas Cromwell, King Henry's chief minister during the dissolution, and in 1538 he gave orders for Sir William Bassett of Langley to dismantle the chapel and Well. This was speedily done, Bassett writing to Lord Cromwell saying, '...*My Lord I have allso lockkyd upp and sealyd the bathys and welles att Buxtone thatt none schall enter...*'[32] and he also took the statue of Saint Anne which was forwarded to Cromwell's place near Austin Friars in London. Sir William Bassett's letter tells us that the chapel contained the offerings of those seeking a cure '...*cruchys, schertes and schetes with wax offered...*'[33] and that he had ordered the keeper that no more offerings should be made. His letter also suggests that the '...*bathys and welles...*' were enclosed otherwise they could not have been sealed up in such a way that no-one could enter.

It is unlikely, however, that they were closed for long for in 1541 a judgment was enacted in Chancery requiring Robert and Roger Cotterell to allow a priest to sing and say mass and other divine service in the chapel of Saint Anne. The Cotterells, as we have noted, came into possession of the land on which the chapel and Well stood in 1489 but in the mid 16th century the family were engaged in a number of disputes over the use of the chapel and Well, and over who should be entitled to the offerings made there. In 1553-55 the Cotterells were charged with preventing the people of Buxton from using the chapel for divine service, as required in the decree of 1541, also locking up the chapel and taking away the key. Furthermore they had allowed youthful persons to wash and bathe themselves in St

Anne's Well, to get drunk within the chapel and to pipe, dance, hop and sing, all to the great disturbance of the inhabitants of Buxton, but, most heinously, to do this on a Sunday. The case was heard at Derby and must have been considered serious by the Justice of Assize for Roger Cotterell was bound over in the sum of £100, a very large amount, and had to pay most of the costs of both sides in the dispute. The Cotterells fought a further case in 1569 from which we learn that they had enjoyed the profits from the Chapel of St. Anne with the Wells adjoining for 60 years, though for much of that time it seems that they had been in dispute with the clergy of Bakewell. However, in this same year they sold the Chapel, well and spring grounds to the sixth Earl of Shrewsbury.[34]

Accounts of the 'miracle cures' obtained did much to enhance the reputation of the well at Buxton in Mediaeval times. The circumstances of a certain Mr Wentworth's visit in about 1560 had significant later implications for his family:

'...One Mr Wentworth of Wentworth Woodhouse, a great Yorkshire landowner, had married and had four daughters. "He fell into a fever and his life was despaired of, and being alone in bed had a vision of a fair woman who said she came from God and that her name was God's Pity. She told him to go to St Anne's Well at Buxton and wash there; she told him things to come which he could not reveal, his wife and mother coming upstairs the vision vanished; he told them of the vision, he went to Buxton and afterwards had a son and saw him grow up to 27." That son told his story to his own son who lived to be the famous Thomas Wentworth, Earl of Strafford, whose execution in 1641 was one of the first signs of the revolt of the Parliament against Charles I. But for his grandfather's visit to Buxton the great Strafford, one of the most striking figures in English history, might never have been born..'[35]

Royal Patronage

In the fourth quarter of the 16th century the fame of Buxton and its waters was greatly enhanced by two sets of circumstances. Firstly, in 1572, Dr John Jones published the first known medical treatise on Buxton waters. Secondly and most importantly, Buxton was visited on several occasions between 1573 and 1584 by Mary Queen of Scots.

Dr John Jones' book was entitled *The Benefit of the auncient Bathes of Buckstones, which cureth most greevous sicknesses, never before published.* He described the situation of Buxton and its natural warm and cold springs, indicating rules for bathing including times, length of stay in the bath and diet. He associated the medicinal virtues of the water with religious belief and set out a lengthy prayer to be said at the bath side as part of the bathing regime. Jones referred to three chief baths and said that the first of these chief baths was the warmer spring. He described the Baths as being '...*bravely beautified with Seats round about, and defended from the ambient air, and chimneys for fire to air your Garments in the Bath side, and other Necessaries most decent..*'[36] though it is not clear if he is describing here all three baths or just the first chief bath. He also described the new Hall being built by the Earl of Shrewsbury and said that this was adjoining the chief spring between the river and the bath. It is reasonable to conclude that, at this time, there was a main bath in use together with two others one of which was St Anne's Well, the other either a bath or a well.

Dr Jones made a number of recommendations. He argued for a permanent physician to be available and he put forward ideas for assisting the poor, the first mention of a bath charity. His claims for cures obtained through the use of the water were extensive and included,

'...Women that by reason of overmuch moisture, or contrary distemperature bee unapt to conceive... weake men that be unfrutefull... profitable for such as have the consumption of the lungs... very good for the inflammation of the liver... it stayeth wasting of man's seede, the Hemoroydes, and Pyles, it soone amendeth... for them that be short winded it much availeth... the greene sickness it perfectly cureth...'.

The book also described the games and pastimes available which included, bowling, shooting, wind or yarne ball (a form of handball) and a game called 'Troule in Madam', which consisted of rolling leather or similar balls into slots, rather like rollerball. Dr Jones dedicated his book to the sixth Earl of Shrewsbury and his Countess Elizabeth (Bess of Hardwick) who were probably his patrons, and this book was undoubtedly an advertisement for Buxton then being developed by the Earl to attract visitors.

In 1569 the sixth Earl of Shrewsbury, George Talbot, was given custody of Mary Queen of Scots, an onerous task which was to occupy him for 15 of the almost 19 years she spent in captivity. During that time the Scottish Queen spent time at Sheffield Castle and Manor with visits to Chatsworth, Tutbury Castle, Wingfield and Buxton. She came to Buxton seeking cures for her illnesses which have been variously described as *'...a severe grief of the splene...'*, digestive upsets, headaches, rheumatism and recurring pain in the side.

The Earl was a major landowner in northern England and had enhanced his property holdings when he married Bess of Hardwick in 1568. He visited Buxton in 1569 seeking treatment for gout in his hands and legs and, from his own report, benefited greatly from taking the waters. Mary Queen of Scots first requested to go to *'Bookston's Well'* in 1571 and she renewed her request in 1572 but Queen Elizabeth would not allow a visit, her reason being that the Hall, then being built by the Earl of Shrewsbury, was not ready.

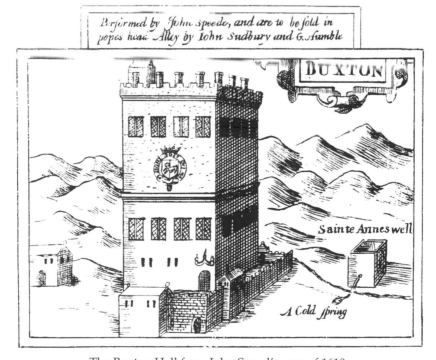

The Buxton Hall from John Speed's map of 1610

Queen Elizabeth was very wary of Mary Queen of Scots who was the natural leader of a large Catholic minority and posed a very real challenge to the English throne. Given the political intrigue and plotting of the time, Buxton, a remote village in the hills, represented a possible safe haven for the Scottish queen and a consequent security risk for Queen Elizabeth. The correspondence between the sixth Earl of Shrewsbury and the royal court, principally Lord Burghley, the Lord Treasurer, reflects the great suspicion with which Queen Elizabeth viewed Mary's visits to Buxton. On 10th August 1573 Lord Burghley wrote to Shrewsbury saying that the queen was content that he should move Mary Queen of Scots to Buxton if he could do so without peril and if strangers could be kept away whilst she was there.

The Scottish queen came to Buxton in August and September of 1573 and from written records we know that she returned in 1574, 1575, 1576, 1580, 1582 and 1584, usually for several weeks in the summer. Like bees around a honey pot she was followed to Buxton by members of the royal court, including very influential figures. Lord Burghley, the Lord Treasurer, visited several times and met with the Earl of Shrewsbury who, whilst fulfilling his duties as Queen Mary's gaoler, took the waters for his gout. Other important visitors included Sir Thomas Smith, Secretary of State; Lady Mildmay, wife of Sir Walter, Chancellor of the Exchequer; Lord Gilbert and Lady Mary Talbot; and Sir Thomas Cecil. The most influential visitor by far, however, was Robert Dudley, Earl of Leicester and favourite of Queen Elizabeth.[37]

The visits of Mary Queen of Scots were greatly enjoyed by her and did much to ease her health and low spirits. In 1580 she begged to be allowed to visit Buxton saying that she had found no remedy better for the complaint in her side. Many of the nobility came for a water cure, the Earl of Sussex, for example, drank three pints a day, increasing daily by one extra pint until he reached eight pints, then reducing by a pint a day back to three pints. The Earl of Leicester was advised, in July of 1576, that wherever he travelled he must, '...*drink Buxton Water twenty days together...*'[38]

The idea of spending time at baths and wells for healing and relaxation purposes was becoming popular amongst the nobility and gentry at this time. It has been suggested that the new habit was becoming an accepted part of the social routine of the elite, with humbler people drawn in their wake and, in this way, the secular holiday was beginning to emerge.[39] Undoubtedly Bess of Hardwick used her considerable business acumen to promote Buxton as a fashionable watering place and it is clear, from correspondence, that Shrewsbury's Hall was very busy during this time when Buxton was enjoying extensive royal patronage. She had a sharp wit, however, for when the Earl of Leicester left Buxton limping (due to a 'boyle' on his leg) she inquired if Buxton sent sound men home halting![40]

However, not all who visited came just to take the waters, some it would seem came for less innocent reasons. Queen Elizabeth was concerned that Mary had too much access to the outside world. She was fearful that Mary would endear herself to the common people so the Earl of Shrewsbury was constantly harried to ensure that the Scottish queen was suitably guarded. In 1576 he was obliged to refute the charge that Mary had too much freedom in being allowed to talk to a cripple at the bath and, writing to Lord Burghley in 1580, he gave examples of his strict surveillance at Buxton. In a later letter he said that he was guarding her circumspectly, as the Queen desired, and added '...*the desire I have to serve my sovereign makes peril and pain a pleasure to me...*'[41]

There is little doubt, however, that intrigue and plotting was taking place in this remote place in the hills. In 1574 two conspirators, Alexander Hamilton and Henry Cockyn, confessed that they were in Buxton at Whitsuntide, and Dr Edward Astlowe, who accompanied the Earl of Sussex to Buxton, was a sympathiser of Mary, later tortured for conspiracy. Buxton may be connected with Mary's ultimate conviction of complicity in the Babington plot which led to her execution at Fotheringhay Castle in 1587. Sir Anthony Babington was a Derbyshire Squire who lived at Dethick. He was a Roman Catholic, a young man fired with zealous enthusiasm for Mary's cause and the leader of a group who planned to dethrone Elizabeth in favour of Mary. The early seeds of this plot could have been sown in Buxton for there is evidence, through the confession of a man named Anthony Tyrell, of a meeting of gentlemen and priests at St. Anne of Buckstones at which a rebellion had been planned. Babington and his conspirators were subsequently tried and put to death.[42]

Much of the evidence we have for Mary Queen of Scots' association with Buxton is in written correspondence but there is one piece which is quite unique in that it consists of messages by her and others scratched on a window in the Hall. The window itself has unfortunately been lost but a copy was kept and '...*Things written in the glasse windowes at Buxstons...*' is now part of the Portland papers at Longleat.[43] The practice of scratching on glass could have been simply a pastime or, conceivably, a way of leaving coded messages for others. The window, which was divided into four columns, contains verse and prose in Latin, French and Greek by Mary; Jaques Nau, her secretary; the Earl of Leicester and others written between 1573 and 1582. The physician to Queen Elizabeth and the Earl of Leicester, Dr Bayley, wrote, 'Hoc tantum scio quod nihil scio', loosely translated *'This much I do know, that I know nothing'*. We might speculate on whether this is false modesty on the part of the doctor or some more cryptic message.[44] The most often quoted of Queen Mary's sayings does not appear on this window but was scratched on her last visit in 1584; it is quite prophetic:

> '....*Buxtona quæ calidæ celebrabere nomine lymphæ*
> *Forte mihi posthac non adeunda, vale.*
> Buxton whose fame thy milk warm waters tell
> Whom I perhaps shall see no more, farewell....'[45]

The popularity of Buxton in Tudor times certainly established the reputation of the spa and the fame of the waters caused large numbers of sick poor to visit. In 1595 the people of the village of Fairfield petitioned Queen Elizabeth for permission to maintain a perpetual chapel and priest, citing as part of their case that they were impoverished partly due to contributing to the upkeep of poor sick people who travelled to the baths at Buxton. Two years later, in the 39th year of Queen Elizabeth an act was passed stipulating that no one resorting to the baths at either Bath or Buxton should be allowed to beg and that poor people should obtain relief from their own parish and travel only with the approval of two Justices of the Peace who were to determine the duration of their visit.

As the reputation of the waters spread, the accommodation at Buxton expanded. In a survey of Derbyshire's taverns and inns in 1577 the only two inns recorded in the High Peak were in Buxton which also had eight ale houses. One of the inns was the Earl of Shrewsbury's new Hall, which was frequented by the nobility. Those of lesser means would, no doubt, have found accommodation in the ale houses or inns which, by 1592, included the Eagle and Child in the higher part of the town, kept by Thomas Downes. Despite this, visitors met difficulties with both accommodation and travel. Sir Thomas Throckmorton experienced very wet weather in the summer of 1594 and decided Bath in Somerset would be better for him. Roger Manners, 5th Earl of Rutland, visiting in 1595, unfortunately saw nothing of commendation apart from the water. Gilbert Talbot, the 7th Earl of Shrewsbury, took the precaution of giving directions for food to be ready on his arrival in September 1609. Lady Arbella Stuart, travelling in the same year, showed great tenacity throughout all of her visit. Proceeding to Chatsworth from Sheffield, she sent pack horses and baggage with six men direct to Buxton. She was guided herself to Buxton by one of Mr Cavendish's men and borrowed four coach horses from her cousin Henry Cavendish to help her coach over the hills. On leaving she was guided over the moors to Sheffield by two men supplied by the Earl of Shrewsbury and, when her coach broke down on the journey, she was obliged to pay the Earl of Pembroke's coachman 10s. for a lift. Added to this was the need to pay workmen to repair the road on the moors which must have been in a very bad state.[46] The reputation of the water and the popularity of Buxton was beginning to emerge but, as we shall see in the next chapter, the amenities and roads did not keep pace with this growing celebrity.

Pooles Cavern, Buxton, from Leigh 1700.

CHAPTER TWO

The Growth of the Spa

From the beginning of the 17th century we see an increasing number of writers describing the waters at Buxton and extolling their virtues. An edition of *Britannia* by the antiquary and historian, William Camden, published in 1607, describes the Buxton Well as *'...being found by experience good for the stomach, nerves, and the whole body. The right honourable George Earl of Shrewsbury has lately erected buildings there, and they have begun to be resorted to by the nobility...'*[1]

Between 1613 and 1622 the poet, Michael Drayton, published an extremely long poem on the history and topography of Great Britain called *Poly-Olbion* and, though much of his information came from Camden's *Britannia*, he offers a fine description of Buxton wells:

'Yet for her caves and holes, Peake onely not excells,
But that I can again produce those wondrous wells
Of Buckston, as I have, that most delicious fount,
Which when the second bath of England doe account
Which in the primer raignes, when first this well began,
To have her vertues knowne unto the blest Saint Anne,
Was consecrated then, which the same temper hath,
As the most daintie spring, which at the famous bath,
Is by the crosse enstild, whose fame I much preferre
In that I doe compare my daintiest spring to her
Nice sickness to cure, as also to prevent,
And supple thier cleare skinnes, which ladies oft frequent;
Most full, most faire, most sweet and most delicious sourse'[2]

The votive coin find of 1975, described in the last chapter, included a token, a coin, jewellery and pins spanning the 17th century, which suggests a continuing line of use of the chief bath described by Dr Jones in 1572. The earliest known picture of the Hall and baths occurs on John Speed's map of Derbyshire 1610. The Hall is shown together with a walled perimeter which, we believe, enclosed the chief bath. St Anne's Well is shown and a further building which may be the well chapel. Speed described nine springs, eight warm and one very cold, which ran from under a fair square building of freestone. About 60 paces away, enclosed with four flat stones, was a well called St Anne's, near to which another very cold spring bubbled up. Justine Paget, a barrister, writing in 1630 confirms the position of the chief bath when he describes the Hall as a pretty little brick house inside which the bath, fed by six hot springs and one cold, was situated in a low room. Since the Hall was not built of brick he is most likely describing the bath building. The poetic account of a visit to Buxton by the clergyman Richard James in 1636 appears to describe how the hot and cold springs were managed at that time:

'...Though when I sawe Saint Anne of Buckstones well
Hot with a chimney; for springs colde and warme
Rising together doe the bathing harme...' [3]

The great English dramatist Ben Jonson drew attention to St Anne's Well in a play written in 1633 for William Cavendish, First Earl of Newcastle and nephew to the First Earl of Devonshire. Jonson created a character, 'Father Fitz-Ale', a learned antiquary of the north who reported 'Saint Anne of Buxton's boiling well' and 'Pooles Hole' in his industrious collection of all the written or reported wonders of the Peak.[4] But the seven wonders of the Peak described by Thomas Hobbes, tutor to the Cavendish family, in a book published about 1636[5] and Charles Cotton's *Wonders of the Peak* did much to publicise the Peak District and the Buxton waters.[6] Cotton's book, in particular, was very popular and had reached its fourth edition by 1699. It has been long thought, mainly due to the writings of Charles Cotton that the Hall had been burnt down in 1670 and was left *'...near a ruin...'* being subsequently rebuilt and enlarged by William, third Earl of Devonshire. A recent study by the Royal Commission on Ancient Buildings has discovered that the majority of the original 1573 walls of the Hall still remain within today's Old Hall Hotel. This would suggest that the earl's rebuild was probably not as

Charles Cotton 1630-87.

extensive as previously thought and was probably confined to work on the roof and the windows.[7] However, Dr Thomas Short, writing sixty years later, suggested that the fire in the Hall destroyed the registers which had preserved for some hundreds of years the accounts of remarkable cures; and the rows of crutches hanging in two large rooms, left by the many lame and sick people who had received help with their ailments.[8]

In 1695/6 Cornelius White, landlord of the Hall and Buxton's first lawyer, made further alterations to the Hall and bath. He repaired the inner bath (referred to as the 'Chief' or 'Great' Bath) and drove a level of over 100 yards long from the bath to the river Wye. This enabled the bath to be drained and washed out with fresh water which made for more hygienic bathing. He also built an outer bath on land to the north of the inner bath, where an old kitchen stood, which was designed for the use of the 'poor and impotent'. It was called 'White's Bath' and though walled round was apparently open to the elements. The outer bath dimensions were seventeen feet long by ten foot two inches wide and the water depth five feet four inches; it was fed by the overflow from the inner bath and, like the former, was fitted with a sluice in order to empty the bath when necessary. Short says that White fixed a pump in this bath to pump off the cold springs whilst ladies were in the bath but, afterwards, made a sough to carry off the springs entirely so that they did not chill the warm water. In addition to these bath alterations White built more apartments, new stables adjoining the Hall, gardens and a bowling green.

Despite these improvements it seems that much was lacking in terms of creature comforts both in the Hall and the bath. The intrepid Celia Fiennes who toured Britain on horseback in 1697 says of the Hall:

'...The beer they allow at the meals is so bad that very little can be dranke..... and sometymes they are so crowded that three must lye in a bed; few people stay above two or three nights its so inconvenient: we staid two nights by reason one of our Company' was ill but it was sore

against our wills, for there is no peace nor quiet with one Company and another going into the Bath or coming out; that makes so many strive to be in this house because the Bath is in it...'

And of the bath house, which she says was '*...about 40 foot long and about 20 or 30 foote broad being almost square... its covered over the top, but not ceiled and there is an open place in the middle like a tunnell, which pours the cold down on your head...'*[9]

This suggests that the bath roof was open to the elements which may have been designed to let out the steam arising from the warm springs. It must certainly have been cold in the bath during the winter especially since the practice of nude bathing had become established.

The young Edward Browne, being a student, stayed in rather more modest accommodation during his journey through the midland counties in September 1662. He wrote: '*...our entertainment was oat cakes and mutton which wee fancied to tastle like dog, our lodging in a low ratty room...'* But he found the waters to be hot and not inferior to those in Somerset.[10]

Both of these travellers found the road to Buxton difficult; Edward Browne was told he had worse hills to go over than any he had passed. Celia Fiennes described her journey from Bakewell:

'*...Its very difficult to find the wayes here for you see only tops of hills and so many roads by reason of the best wayes up and down that its impossible for Coach or Wagon to pass some of them, and you scarce see a tree and no hedges all over the Country, only dry stone walls that incloses ground no other fence. Buxton we saw 2 or 3 tymes and then lost the sight of it as often, and at last did not see it till just you came upon it - that 9 mile we were above 6 hours going it...'*

The most influential 17th century visiting physician was Sir John Floyer of Lichfield whose book on the hot, cold and temperate baths in England, published in 1697, was devoted mainly to Buxton waters. He wrote:

'*...Their stay in the bath is an hour or more, till everyone finds themselves very cool... but no body catches cold, tho they go in naked but I think men ought to use drawers and the women shifts of linen or flannel. But custom hath taught the sexes to have separate times of bathing...'*[11]

Floyer recommended a period of treatment at the Buxton bath of one week during which a diet of flesh meats and moderate drinking was prescribed. Bathing was recommended early in the morning and in the early evening, followed by the drinking of the water. Great claims were made by him regarding the success of his treatments citing successful cures for cases of 'leprosy, dropsie, lameness, pains, gravel and stone'. Floyer's book contains a list of successful water cures carried out by himself but much doubt must lie with his claims. Some people did undoubtedly experience relief from their symptoms and, occasionally, a complete cure, but it could be argued that this was due as much to the imposed regime of abstinence as the taking of the waters themselves.

Floyer was a friend of Dr Charles Leigh of Oxford University, who published a folio book on the natural history of Lancashire, Cheshire and the Peak in Derbyshire in 1700. Leigh describes

Charles Leigh, Doctor of Physick.

experiments which he did with Floyer on the chalybeate water at Buxton and these two eminent men give us our first introduction to this iron bearing water, which we describe more fully later. Both writers refer to the bath which we take to be the chief bath and so we may firmly identify at least three sources of water in use at this time, the chief bath, St Anne's Well and a chalybeate well, though, given Dr Jones' earlier description, there may have been other springs in use.

At the close of the 17th century Dr Charles Leigh reflected the growing recreation of spa bathing when he wrote of the Peak District...

'...She liberally affords Hot and mineral waters, for the Relief and Comfort of infirm and decrepit Mortals; so that these untractable and dispeopl'd Parts become frequented with numerous Crouds, who yearly arrive here, either through a Prospect of Ease from their Pains and Infirmities, or for the pleasing Entertainment of the Mind with new Objects, of which these parts are very prolifick...' [12]

New Drinking Well

In 1709 Sir Thomas Delves (1632-1713) of Doddington Hall in Cheshire was so satisfied with his successful treatment using the Buxton waters that he decided to commemorate his cure by erecting a stone alcove over the existing drinking well dedicated to St Anne in the yard, some 25 yards north of the outer bath. In so doing he demolished the old Roman well whose remains were lost to us from that time. Delves' new well building was about twelve feet square and surrounded on its inside walls with stone benches. It had one of its four sides open to the outside with a strong bar across it to strengthen the arched roof. Inside the water rose into a stone basin in the middle of the structure.

Barker's Bath

Possibly because of the poor roofing facilities at the baths, as described by Celia Fiennes, William, the second Duke of Devonshire (1673-1729), commissioned the architect, John Barker of Rowsley, to reconstruct the baths and other buildings adjacent to the Hall. The scheme involved the construction of a stone vault roof over the bath to protect the bathers from inclement weather. The contract was to be completed by May 1712 at a cost of £400. Barker had earlier worked at Belvoir Castle and Chatsworth upon such buildings as the stables. The facade shows the clear influence of this previous work with a row of three bulls-eye windows which were a common feature in stable architecture.[13]

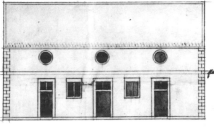

The main inner bath (also referred to as the 'Chief' or 'Great' bath) was described by Dr Thomas Short, writing in 1734 as twenty six feet six inches long by

John Barker's plans of 1710/12 for new baths at the Hall

twelve feet eight inches wide with a water depth of four foot nine inches at the lower end and four foot three inches at the head. The bath room he described as:

'...A large stately arch room, ten yards long, five yards and a half wide, and much the same height. There is a stone bench along one end and side of it, for the bathers to dress and undress upon; between this and the bath is a walk of smooth flagstones, and at the corners of the bath, at each end, are very good stone steps or stairs to go down.... At the north or lower end, is a large square hole in the foundations of the house wall, which gives vent to the water out of this into the outer bath...'[14]

Intriguingly, the Bodleian Library at Oxford possesses a sketch titled 'Buxton Bath Derbyshire, July 1712' which at first sight appears to be another and perhaps stylised view of the Barker barrel-roofed inner bath. Closer examination however shows that the sketch does not have any windows on either of its long walls whereas external elevations of 1710-12 and another internal sketch of the inner bath as it appeared in 1807 clearly show three windows in its south wall. It is tempting to surmise that this sketch shows the outer bath with the two entrances on its left wall leading from the inner bath. However, as we have seen from Dr. Short's description, the outer bath was still unroofed in 1734. We conclude that the Bodleian Library sketch gives a view of the Barker bath looking east.[15]

Access to Buxton and its accommodation continued to present difficulties for travellers in the early 18th century. In 1704 Bishop William Nicholson travelled on a good road from Manchester to Whaley Bridge but from there to Buxton the road was mountainous and rough, and in 1708 a large party from Lyme Hall found the same road wild and uneven. A year before, Lady Pye visiting lent her coach to some ladies: *'...Who so well louded it that it quite unjointed and fell to pieces past mending...'*[16]

Daniel Defoe, author of *Robinson Crusoe* published his *Tour through the Whole Islands of Great Britain* in three volumes between 1724 and 1726 but he may have visited Buxton some time before this. His journey in from the south was good *'...entring upon Brassington Moor... we had eight mile smooth green riding to Buxton Bath...'* and he found the accommodation good but limited and, like Edward Browne before him, compared Buxton favourably against Bath in Somerset:

'...The Duke of Devonshire is Lord of the village, and consequently of the bath itself; and his grace has built a large handsome house at the bath, where there is convenient lodging, and very good provisions, and an ordinary well served for one shilling per head; but it is but one. And although some other houses in the town take in lodgers upon occasion, yet the conveniences are not the same; so that there is not accommodation for a confluence of people, as at the Bath-house itself; if it were otherwise, and that the Nobility and Gentry were suitably entertained, I doubt not but Buxton would be frequented, and with much more effect as to health, as well as much more satisfaction

Buxton Bath July 1712

to the company; where there is an open and healthy country, a great variety of view to satisfy the curious, and a fine down or moor for the ladies to take a ring upon in their coaches, and much more convenient than in a close city as the Bath is, where may be said to stink like a general common [sewer]...' [17]

Sketch of Barker's bath as it existed in 1807

So Buxton offered much clearer air than its rival Bath! Road improvements were on the way for in 1724 an Act was passed for the repairing and widening of the road from Sherbrook Hill near Buxton to Chapel-en-le-Frith and on through Stockport to Manchester. This turnpike was intended to improve a road: *'...very ruinous, and many Parts thereof almost impassable in the Winter Season, and in divers Places so narrow, that it is become dangerous to Persons passing through the same...'* [18]

A further act of 1729-30 amended the tolls to take account of the large increase in wheeled vehicles using the roads. The road south from Buxton was turnpiked as part of an act of 1751 when the extension from Sherbrook Hill to Hurdlow House (now known as the Bull i' th Thorn Hotel) completed the Manchester to Derby route. Dr Thomas Short, travelling in about 1732 found an easy open road from Buxton to Matlock Bath, perhaps on the parish roads via Chelmorton and Sheldon as the Buxton to Ashford turnpike was not opened until 1812.[19]

Interior of the Bull i' Th Thorn Inn.

There is some evidence of a significant extension of the Hall between 1725 and 1734. As part of this it has been suggested that the incumbent landlord, Mr Taylor, may have built a new ladies bath in about 1726.[20] However this is not borne out by Short who does not describe a separate ladies bath in his 1734 history, though, as we have seen, he does mention the use of the outer bath by ladies. In fact it is not until 50 years later that three baths are first identified.

Short does describe some of the entertainments provided for the visitor to the baths. He remarks upon the variety of game to be found on the moors and the good fishing in the river Wye and goes on:

'...And Mr Taylor of the Hall upon his own Expenses, keeps a very good pack of hounds, for Gentlemans' Diversion, as also a pleasant warm Bowling Green planted about with large Sycamore trees; and in the House a fine English and French Billiard Table. A little East of St Anne's Well, over the Ditch or Level which carries the Warm water from the Bath, is made a curious natural hot Bed, and upon the rest of this Canal might be made the finest Greenhouse in the Northern Kingdoms; he has also taken in several new Gardens with planting, and several curious Walks...' [21]

So it would seem that the amenities had improved considerably since the time of Daniel Defoe.

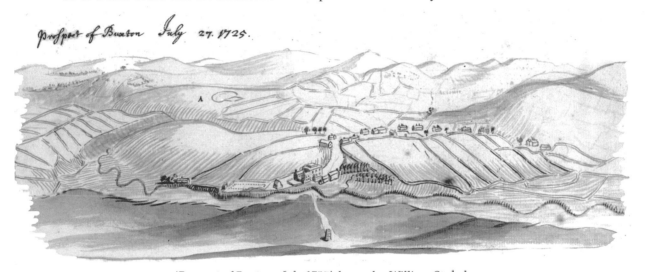

'Prospect of Buxton - July 1725' drawn by William Stukeley.

The Springs

Short's book carries a detailed description of the positioning of the town's main springs. It is not possible to vouch for the accuracy of his description but he was in the fortunate position of being able to actually see the springs before the Crescent and baths were built over them. His description provides important evidence and is summarised here:

1. Several warm springs arising through the floor of the [Great] Bath.

2. St Ann's Well, 32.5 yards north east of the Bath, supplied by a spring on its north side, rising through black limestone or bastard marble under a shelving stone laid for that purpose.

3. A hot and a cold spring, both rising into the same receptacle in a close 20 yards south east of St Ann's Well.

4. Bingham (or Mr Leigh's) Well, 63 yards south, south east of St Ann's well.

5. Small hot spring, a little way east of Bingham Well, with an adjacent cold spring.

6. Another warm spring 34 yards east of St Ann's Well situated in the stream of the level which carries the water from the [Great] Bath.

7. Four yards further east and on the south side of this stream rise two or three other warm springs.[22] Of these springs it would seem that at least three were used for drinking, having bowls or receptacles over the spring to collect the water. One of these was Bingham Spring which was described by Short as Mr Leigh's Well and in his contents page, though not in the main text, as St Peter's Well. Very little documented evidence for this well exists today and we are unable to ascertain whether the well was run as an organised concern or whether it was patronised on a more casual basis. Certainly, Dr Short attached some importance to this source since it is referred to in his writings in almost equal measure as the thermal spring water. Unlike the main springs the water flow from the Bingham spring varied according to the seasons, indicating that the spring probably did not originate from any great depth. The origin of the name Bingham is also unknown but the alternative name of Leigh's Well can be traced to a Mr Leigh of Lyme Hall who was a regular user of the well. By the start of the 19th century this well had ceased to be used though it is possible that the water source was 'rediscovered' at the time of the 1851-54 rebuild of the baths. It is thought that the source of Bingham's Well is, today, buried under a manhole in the middle of the road between the Pump Room and the east wing of the Crescent.

Dr Short's writing also gives an insight into the medical rationale of the time with his description of how the healing waters enter the body. He wrote;

'...since the waters can penetrate the bather's skin, via the pores, surely it follows that they can find a passage between the fibres making up the sides of blood vessels and thus remove any obstructions which may be present and expell them...'

The premise on which the above hypothesis is based relies on the universally held belief of the time, that the skin was to some degree porous and allowed the water, together with its minerals to enter the body. Nowadays it is recognised that although absorption of liquid is to a degree experienced through the upper layers of the epidermis (particularly the palms of the hands and the soles of the feet) absorption of a degree likely to make sufficient difference to the functioning of the bodily organs seems very unlikely.

The 17th and 18th century medical men had very little in terms of effective drugs with which to fight infections and illnesses of all types. There was a general unawareness of the need for hygiene in the fight against bacterial infections and consequently death rates were relatively high and life span correspondingly short. Because of the lack of specific drugs to fight disease, great emphasis was made of what they did have - sources of pure water. Bathing in and drinking of Buxton water was trumpeted as a cure for all conditions no matter how serious. Dr Short, for example, sets out a long catalogue of the complaints which may be cured by Buxton water, in most, but not all, cases he advised both drinking and bathing.

'...Upon the whole, Buxton Water being warm, highly impregnated with a mineral stream, vapour or spirit, containing a most subtle and impalpable Sulphur, and being the product of Limestone; it is therefore rarefying, heating, relaxing, thinning, sweetening, and a little drying, hence it is signally beneficial, and surprisingly successful in the Gout, Rheumatism, scorbutic and arthritic Pains, wandering or fixt Pains

inveterate or recent; Cramps, Convulsions, dry Asthma's without a Fever or quick Pulse, bilious Cholick, want of Appetite and Indigestion from Intemperance, hard drinking &c. Contractions, Stiffness and Lameness therefrom in any Part, Barrenness from a Constriction and idilatibility of the Fallopian Tubes and Uterus.... Ringworms, Scab, Itch, for scouring off Sand, Sludge and Gravel out of the Kidneys...'[23]

Cure seekers of the Georgian era were not known for their personal cleanliness and many suffered from chronic skin diseases so it is scarcely surprising that some experienced a degree of improvement in their condition since an annual or biannual bath in any type of water was likely to be beneficial.

Buxton Rivals Bath

Improved road access during the latter half of the 18th century saw a large increase in the fashion of taking the waters led, in the most part, by the city of Bath with its naturally warm springs. The fifth Duke of Devonshire who owned the Buxton baths was concerned that the popularity of Buxton and

THE

NATURAL, EXPERIMENTAL, and MEDICINAL

HISTORY

OF THE

MINERAL WATERS

OF

Derbyshire, Lincolnshire, and Yorkshire,

Particularly those of

SCARBOROUGH.

WHEREIN,

They are carefully examined and compared, their Contents discovered and divided, their Uses shewn and explained, and an Account given of their Discovery and Alterations.

Together with the

NATURAL HISTORY of the EARTHS, MINERALS and FOSSILS through which the Chief of them pass.

THE

Groundless Theories, and False Opinions of former WRITERS are exposed, and their Reasonings demonstrated to be injudicious and inconclusive.

To which are added,

Large MARGINAL NOTES, containing a Methodical Abstract of all the Treatises hitherto published on these WATERS, with many OBSERVATIONS and EXPERIMENTS.

AS ALSO

Four Copper-Plates representing the Crystals of the Salts of Thirty four of those Waters.

By *THOMAS SHORT*, M. D. of *Sheffield.*

Aqua Fontana limpida ad Sanitatem conservandam saluberrima, ad amissam recuperandam Mineralis præstantissima.

LONDON,

Printed for the AUTHOR, and sold by F. GYLES over against *Gray's Inn* in *Holborn*, M DCC XXXIV.

Title page of Thomas Short's book 1734

its waters might suffer, particularly as the Royal Crescent, the New Assembly Rooms and the rebuilding of the Hot baths was undertaken at Bath between 1767 and 1777 by the architect John Wood the younger.

At Buxton Dr Hunter, writing in 1768, still describes only one bath in existence (he may not have considered a bath for the use of the poor worthy of mention since at the time it was in a neglected condition) but by 1784 Dr Pearson describes an additional bath for the use of ladies which was situated '...adjoining the old bath now appropriated to the men, called the Gentlemen's Bath...'[24]

It can be safely assumed that this was the large ladies bath which existed before the addition of the four baths by John Carr which we describe below. It is likely also that this bath would not have been open to the elements, therefore a bath building adjacent to that housing the Great Bath must have been built to accommodate it.

Despite this extra bath the Buxton baths were inadequate for the increasing numbers seeking treatment and the duke entered into discussions with a well known northern architect, John Carr of York (1723-1807) with a view to enlarging the facilities. These discussions came to a head sometime between 1777 and 1779 and Carr was commissioned to undertake the improvements as suggested by the Duke of Devonshire. Carr was himself a sufferer of rheumatism, being greatly troubled by back and leg pain, and had taken the Buxton water cure in 1775 with some degree of relief. Carr's plans for the baths renovation are impressive, featuring one round and three oval baths within a new building immediately to the east of the existing baths. The outside of the new baths was to boast an Ionic colonnade between two elegant Ionic pavilions with a frontage of 75 feet 6 inches in length. Unfortunately Carr had to abandon his elaborate new bath plans due to the difficulties encountered in gaining permission to build the Crescent on land to the north of the baths. The problems proved too difficult to overcome and it was eventually decided to build the Crescent on the site which had been allocated to the new baths. [25]

This resulted in the building of an alternative and probably cheaper set of four new baths within the existing bath complex. They were designed by Carr and a detailed analysis of his building accounts suggest they were the Gentlemen's Private, the Ladies Private, the Matlock and the Cold Bath. Work commenced with the digging of drains early in 1786. Some of the new baths were built on land previously occupied by a yard containing shops and it was necessary to pull down these shops before work could commence on the sinking of the baths.

A typical entry in Carr's building accounts details the digging out of the new gentlemen's Private Bath and the payment of four men for their work.

> '... Dec 24 1787.
> To sinking for the Gents Private Bath taking the steps out of Gents old Bath beside the pump...
>> Willm. Eyre 6 days, 9 shillings.
>> William Fletcher 6 days, 8 shillings.
>> Jn Bennett 6 days, 8 shillings
>> Jn Needam Three quarters of a day, 1 shilling...' [26]

John Carr's building accounts of 1787 also refer to '...letting in irons at the Ladies bath to hang the chair in...' which indicates the early use of a chair for lowering invalids into the water. Presumably this facility was not limited to the Ladies Bath and was also available for the gentleman bathers.

The baths were probably completed and in use by 1788 and some part of the yard still remained after the conversions which was used as drying space for the bath towels. Although probably much renovated during the changes, the Great Bath and the Ladies bath remained in their original positions. The Poor Bath was removed and re-sited to the north of the new Matlock Bath and a covered way linking the arcades of the Square and the Crescent to the baths was built. Access to the baths could then be obtained through an archway in the arcade.

Dr Joseph Denman's detailed description of the complete provision in 1793 includes the four new baths, numbers 2,4,5 and 7:

1. The Gentlemen's Bath. The original and oldest bath, 27 feet long by 17 feet wide. It was lined with polished gritstone and paved with the same and there was a pump at its south east corner. The bath had been decreased in size by a reservoir let into it to supply other baths in the complex. The reservoir was 7 feet 6 inches by 4 foot 6 inches. It had a depth of 4 feet 10 inches and a sough at its north end

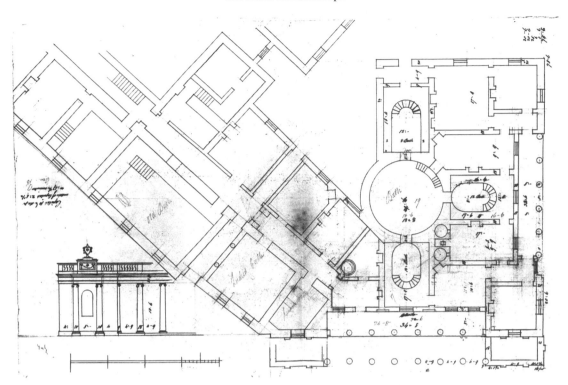

Plan of John Carr's intended new Buxton baths

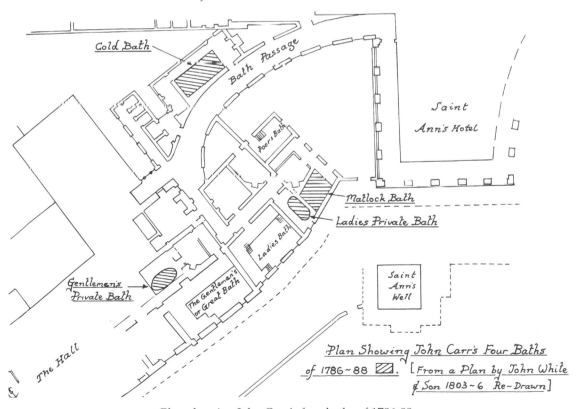

Plan showing John Carr's four baths of 1786-88

through the wall leading to the river which was used to empty the bath daily for cleaning purposes.

2. The Gentlemen's Private Bath. Situated to the south-east, and very near to the Gentlemen's Bath. This bath had an adjoining dressing room through which one passed on the way to the bath. It was oval in form, lined with grey marble and measured 10 feet 6 inches by 6 feet. The water to this bath was fed via lead pipes from the reservoir in the Gentlemen's Bath. On its travel from the other bath the water lost some of its temperature and the Gentlemen's Private Bath was fitted with flues underneath which could raise the water temperature by many degrees. This is perhaps the earliest mention of the temperature of the water being raised artificially though, as we shall see later, the Tonic Bath also had a similar heating arrangement at about this time.

3. The Ladies Public Bath. This was north of and immediately adjoining the Gentlemen's Bath, measuring 22 feet by 12 feet and made of gritstone. The water for this bath rose principally from a number of small springs in various parts of the bath floor and was supplemented by water from the main baths reservoir.

4. The Ladies Private Bath. Next to the previous bath, made of grey marble and oval in shape, and measuring 11 by 4 feet. This bath was supplied with water from the main reservoir.

5. The Matlock Bath. This measured 11 feet 6 inches by 10 feet and was supplied by two lead pipes, one from the warm reservoir and the other from a cold (or possibly chalybeate) spring. By this method the water could be regulated to the temperature of 68°F (19.8°C) the same as that at the fashionable Matlock spring.

6. The Poor Bath. Measuring 8 feet square and supplied by the water overflow from the Gentlemen's Bath and made of gritstone.

All the previous six baths were provided with a 'convenient pump', which we take to mean a douche hose used by attendants to spray the bathers during treatments in the baths.

7. A Bath situated Close to the river Wye. Measuring 15 feet by 10 feet and probably fed from a chalybeate spring with a water temperature of 54°F (12.2° C), it was known as the Cold Bath. The river was arched over to provide flat ground for the building of this bath.

Denman further describes a tepid fountain or drinking well enclosed within the baths building, called the Hall Well. It was enclosed in a room opening into the corridor leading from the Hall to the Crescent. It is possible that this was the temporary well erected during the demolition and rebuilding of St Anne's well by John Carr.[27]

The exterior of the baths building also underwent changes. If the baths exterior as designed by Barker (1712) was carried out as planned, with its two storey design and bull's eye windows, there must have been substantial changes made as engravings from1795 onwards show three adjoining buildings housing the baths. The building adjacent to the Hall is shown as a 3 bay, 3 storey block with windows at eaves level and the upper floors forming part of the Hall. To the side of this were two further buildings, both of two storeys. Comparing this facade with the plan of Carr's baths of 1786-88 we can suggest, with some certainty, that the three storey building housed the Great Bath and the Gentlemen's Private Bath, the middle two storey building housed the Ladies Bath and the third building contained the Ladies Private, the Matlock, the Poor and the Cold Baths. Denman's previous reference to a tepid fountain suggests that the Hall had direct access to the baths and it would also seem that these exterior changes took place as part of Carr's improvements.

The Bath houses in 1804 can be seen on the left of this engraving

From this time the baths returned a useful clear profit under the supervision of John Brandreth who rented a house in the Crescent. The accounts from 1790 show a consistent clear profit of about £700 each year up to the end of the century, rising to a height of £1079 in 1803. His successor was Richard Loft but Brandreth's widow continued to live in the house in the Crescent.[28]

Visitor Accommodation

Although the Hall was certainly a most sought after dwelling place for visitors to the town it was by no means the only hostelry in the area. In addition to the many privately run houses offering food and accommodation there were other hotels most notably, the George Inn and the Grove Coffee House which offered rooms as well as refreshment. On the Market Place was the White Hart and, across the road the Eagle & Child. From 1711 the Shakespeare Inn in Spring gardens offered its hospitality to all visitors. Thomas Nicholson, a Liverpool merchant wrote in September 1807 from the Shakespeare

'We got here about 8 o'clock yesterday evening, and could not be taken in the Grove Inn as it was quite full of company, and after some time took our abode here; I was obliged to sleep out two nights. We dined 24 persons on our arrival which number has fluctuated frequently we have been only 8 and are now 14... The company has furnished variety, none disagreeable; a few rather agreeable, but nothing superlatively so. We pass the time rather pleasantly. I have drank the water moderately and have bathed four times, with benefit I hope, as I walk much farther without fatigue than I should have done on leaving home, but had some unpleasant sensations intimating rheumatism, gout or something I should like to part with.' [29]

Leisure Activities

The baths were an important aspect of the new facilities at Buxton, the main feature of which was John Carr's impressive Crescent with the accompanying stables. The Crescent was designed to provide two hotels, an assembly room and card rooms, six lodging houses and a number of shops, all under the one roof. Adjacent were the newly modernised suite of baths. Thus a whole new leisure complex was created with the Buxton air and the bathing providing an invigorating experience for the visitor. Whilst it may be said that Buxton did not reach the heights of elegance enjoyed by its rival Bath, it could, nevertheless, offer an extensive range of

An assembly in full swing

entertainment. Music and dancing is recorded in the town from the middle of the 18th century and an anonymous poem refers to the use of at least one string instrument.

'...Till health restored forbids your longer stay.
and the brisk fiddle speeds you on your way...'

Despite the fact that many of the visitors to the town were seeking treatment for arthritic and similar conditions there were obviously a sufficient number amongst them who were fit enough to dance together with others of their family. Dancing was regularly held in the evenings, although it seems the arrangements were not to everybody's satisfaction as recorded by a Mrs Stapylton in the 1750s:-

'... [Visitors] sup at eight, and dance till eleven
if you can, but it is with difficulty a set is to be
made up, for it is not approved of for those who
come for their health, and there are not many
here upon any other account...'

Balls were held in various hotels, the most popular of which was the long room of the Hall. As late as 1789 we are informed that *'...when a dance is intended at any one of the houses, it is usual to send cards of invitation to the company who lodge in other parts of the village, and those who wish to join in the amusement assemble immediately after supper...'*

After the erection of the Crescent the balls were almost always held in the Assembly Room on the first floor of the east wing of the building which, as well as a superb dancing and meeting place, also provided adjacent coffee and card rooms. The balls attracted a great many distinguished and titled guests as well as the middle and upper class customers. Several contemporary writings refer to the comparatively small number of gentlemen compared to ladies attending the balls for various reasons including exhaustion after grouse shooting on the surrounding moorland. The well stocked rivers around the area also provided sport for the visiting gentlemen who preferred to spend their time fishing for trout and grayling.[30] Miss Seaward makes reference to the low male representation in August 1798, due, undoubtedly, to the war with France and the Napoleonic threat to British soil:

'...The crowd is immense, though I never remember so few families of rank, and there is a trustful lack of elegant beaux. The male youth and middle life of England are, as you know, all soldiered and gone to camps and coasts; and so a few prim parsons and a few dancing doctors are the forlorn hopes of the belles...' [31]

Imagine the scene at these great balls, with elegantly dressed ladies and gentlemen dancing under the elaborate Adamite ceiling of the Crescent Assembly Room lit by candlelight from the three ornate glass chandeliers and wall candle holders. The scene would have been further enhanced on winter evenings when the two great fireplaces would have provided both heat and a further source of flickering light to the dancing company.

From at least 1784 the visitor was able to visit the theatre. Buxton's first recorded purpose-built theatre was in Spring Gardens and although the building has been described in unflattering terms by visitors it appears to have been better inside than out. Despite these restrictions the theatre was well attended and the typical format of an evening started with the main entertainment followed by a comic song or dance and concluded almost invariably with a farce. The Spring

Guests arriving at the Crescent by coach

Gardens Theatre was closed or demolished in 1829 and was replaced by another theatre at the lower end of Hall Bank in 1833. [32]

A popular attraction throughout the history of Buxton has been the natural show cave of Poole's Cavern at the foot of Grin Woods. Today the cave is well lit and has an enlarged entrance and even access for disabled people in wheelchairs. Back in the 18th century the cave experience was considerably more threatening. Stukeley describes the cave in 1725:

'...About half a mile off is that stupendous cavern called Pool's Hole, under a great mountain: the entrance at the foot thereof is very low and narrow, so that you must stoop to get in: but immediately it dilates into a wide and lofty concavity, which reaches about a quarter of a mile end-wide and farther, as they tell us: some old women with lighted candles are guides in this Cimmerian obscurity: water drops from the roof every where, and incrusts all the stones with long crystals and fluors: whence a thousand imaginary figures are shown you, by the name of lions, fonts, lanterns, organs, flinch of bacon etc...'

The animal and other references above relate to the strange rock formations formed on the walls, floor and ceiling of the cave, by years of water ingress through the limestone terrain. These formations are still visible today and are largely known by the same names. [33]

Not all of the visiting health seekers were sufficiently infirm to forbid a walk in the surrounding hills and many used their leisure time in this way. A popular walking attraction was to be found at Lovers Leap in Ashwood Dale, a naturally occurring deep chasm in the limestone. Colonel Byng, during a visit to the town tells of his walking experiences in the area; *'...In the evening I strolled a walk, not deficient in wild beauty, above the stream, where is a hew of rocks, and a profundity, sufficient to astonish a Londoner.*

I often sat to view them, but in pensiveness; and so I started up for exercise, and new objects. No fat man can walk in this country, as the upright stone stiles are so narrow, as only to admit the passage of a well sized leg..." [34]

Can we conclude from this piece that Byng was something of a corpulent fellow? One diversion in town, cockfighting, has a long history recorded as far back as 1580. Some of the town's visitors would have taken time to witness the spectacle and doubtless have placed bets on the result of a fight to the death of one of the unfortunate fowls. One known cockpit was on the site of the present Methodist Church on the Market Place. When the church was built in 1849 the Buxton Herald remarked

'...If progress depends on the substitution of piety and learning for barbarism and ignorance then we are assuredly on the right road for the chapel is on the site of the Buxton cockpit where the great mains between Lancashire and Yorkshire were formerly fought. Let us hope that this metamorphosis is not accidental that it is a mere material illustration of the improved morals and habits of the people...' [35]

Time and money could be dwindled away in any of the many shops. Retailers made very good use of the unique geology of the area and produced ornaments and trinkets from the various types of fluorstone available, the most famous being the multicoloured Blue John. Buxton sported many such souvenir shops. The spar material could be turned and carved into elaborate pieces ranging from

Blue John vases typical of the spa ornaments sold in Buxton shops in the 18th and 19th centuries

jewellery to large decorative vases.

B. Faujas St. Fond describes the thriving businesses in the town in 1799:-

'...*Several artists in this line have settled at Buxton on account of the numerous and in general opulent visitants who resort thither for the waters, and whole fancy or taste inclines them to purchase their productions. The fluor spars are turned into small hollow or solid vases, columns, eggs, pears, and watches. and cut into pyramids, pedestals, &c. As the colours are beautiful and variegated, and the stone is susceptible of a fine shining polish, it was formerly sold at a very high rate; but since it has been found in so great abundance, the increase of artificers, and the consequent competition among each other, have contributed to diminish very much the price of these articles of ornament. There are very few among the stonecutters of Buxton who show any taste for the beautiful forms. They have signs above their shop doors with their names and the addition of petrifaction-works.*

The most intelligent of them, in my opinion, was one Noel, who was in easy circumstances, and had succeeded well in his branch of trade. He was bringing up to the same art a daughter and a son, who were almost as well skilled as himself, though the boy was only eight, and the girl nine years of age. It was at his shop that the best turned vases were to be seen.

Samuel Cooper had the best stocked shop; but his pieces were dearer than those of the others.

John Evens and Mottershead, are two other artificers who have pretty good assortments...'

He continues to refer to the main source of the fluorspar:

'...*The fluorspar, which is fashioned at Buxton, is procured from the lead mines of Castellation* [Castleton], *about ten miles from the former. The only stones of value found in the environs of Buxton, are a very fine gypsies, white, semitransparent alabaster, which is made into vases and pedestals, a black marble emitting a bituminous smell on being rubbed, and a yellowish calcareous spar, both of which are applied* to the same purpose...'[36]

The same materials are still used to fashion trinkets, mostly jewellery, today. The material is becoming more difficult to mine economically and hence smaller amounts are extracted. This inevitably means that large articles can no longer be produced but some superb examples still remain on display in the local museum.

Chalybeate Water

In addition to the natural thermal springs Buxton had at least one chalybeate or iron-containing water spring (pronounced kal-i-be-at). In common with most other chalybeate waters the spring arose from a bed of shale. An early mention of this spring was made by Dr Charles Leigh in 1700 who said that a mixture of the Buxton thermal and chalybeate waters closely approximated the healing properties imparted by the waters of Bath in Somerset and of St Vincent's near Bristol.

Dr Allen, writing in 1711 mentions a chalybeate spring '...*not far off...*" [the baths] and Dr Short (1734) describes the same chalybeate source '... *on the north side of the brook, opposite the Hall...*' and also recommends the mixing of the thermal spring water or Bingham Well water with the chalybeate to be used as a gentle purgative. He goes on to say '...*it is pretty clear as it rises, but lets fall much oker in its basin and stream, weighs pretty near the same with common water, lays the spirits in the thermometer one eighth of an inch lower than the river. It has a nauseous, rough and irony taste...*'[37]

The oker referred to here is the orange/red ferrous deposit or sinter found at the outlet of most chalybeate springs.

Dr Denman (1793) also talks of the chalybeate spring, describing its position as north of the river and immediately below the George Inn. He complains about its polluted appearance due to the recent construction of the Crescent:

'...*Besides the tepid springs which are peculiar to Buxton, there is also a chalybeate, which rises from a bank of shale on the north side of the river, and immediately below the George inn. this spring, before the building of the Crescent, was a clear water, and much in use. Doubtless, at the time of covering the river for the purpose of erecting the Crescent with its offices, the intention was to preserve and improve this spring; as is evident from the neat little dome placed over it. By some means, however, either from the enlargement of the surface, by which it is become more exposed to the common air; or from some other cause, the water is now always in a state of decomposition, muddy and unfit for use..*'[38]

Buxton's chalybeate water emerged from the spring at a temperature of 54°F (12.2°C). It was referred to as 'mild' and was used for eye bathing and as a general tonic.

New Drinking Well

The building of the Crescent (1780-89) made it necessary to demolish the drinking well built by Delves in 1709. Under the terms of the Enclosure Act (1773-74) the Duke of Devonshire was obliged by law to provide public access to the waters and John Carr was commissioned to build a new drinking well to be sited at the foot of the slopes. For the duration of the building work a temporary well was erected at the southern corner of the Hall. The new well was completed in January 1783 with water being piped from the site of the old well which was demolished in March 1783. The new well was described by Jewitt in 1811:

'...*A beautiful square building in the Grecian style, three sides of which have three semi-circular niches to serve as resting places for the water drinkers; the fourth, which is the entrance, is closed with a door of open iron work. this side, which is the front, is supported by two columns of the Tuscan order, and the whole building is surmounted by a beautiful urn...*' [39]

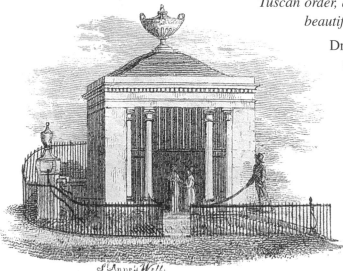

Drinking Well by John Carr

Dr George Pearson, writing in 1784 describes the interior of the new well;

'...*the basin of the new St Anne's well is hewn out of one entire mass of gritstone, and it is covered with a massy stone of the same kind, placed in contact with the water and cemented down. An aperture is made in the side of the basin through which the water perpetually flows as from a pump spout, at the rate of half a pint in a second of time. A neat basin of white marble is placed under the stream that flows through the aperture, for the convenience of filling glasses and other vessels with this water...*'[40]

St Anne's Well Women

Another stipulation of the Enclosure Act was that St Anne's well should be kept clean and in good repair. After 1773/4, in order to comply with this, the Vestry (an early form of local government) appointed a well woman annually to look after the well and dispense the water to the public. The act appears to have formalised an already existing arrangement since an anonymous writer of 1769 records that a young female attended to dip the water. Further evidence for this assertion exists on the gravestone of Martha Brandreth at St Peter's Churchyard, Fairfield which reads:

'...HERE lieth the remains of JOB BRANDRETH , who departed this life Dec. 24th 1775, aged 60 years. Also to the memory of MARTHA BRANDRETH. relict of the above, Who during a series of Fifty years with skilful and attentive Hand administered the waters of The celebrated Fountain at Buxton. When To forbear or use the Baths she understood, And free, tho' not familiar, when asked she spoke her Mind among the various classes of a numerous Publick resorting to the Place, and amidst her Neighbours she lived Respected, and by all lamented, DIED on the 8th day of June, 1795. aged 81 years. Here rest her remains...' [41]

Martha Brandreth was never listed as being appointed by the Vestry. Although the annual appointment was for one woman it is likely that the total compliment was more than one, if only to cover during periods of sickness. The appointed woman served for one year only and names were changed often. Another well woman, the venerable Martha Norton was elected to the post fifteen times between 1775-1820, a period of 46 years if we are to assume her continuous attendance at both the Delves and the Carr well. [42]

The well designed by John Carr was in use throughout the first half of the 19th century and continued to be staffed by well women annually by the Vestry. In 1818 the Vestry appointed Peggy Brandreth and set out duties for her and the other women. These included helping the poor women in the Charity Bath, cleaning out the bath and drying mats, bathing gowns and towels. In 1822 there were three well women and, since they were not paid but relied on tips for income, we cannot be certain whether they fulfilled the duties set out. It is, perhaps, not surprising that in 1840 the Buxton Bath Charity resolved to appoint their own female Charity Bath attendant. The well women supplemented their income by selling articles at the well, though this was stopped in 1842. After the major rebuilding of the baths in 1851-54 the well women worked in the new pump room which was part of the Natural Baths complex. In 1872, they were allowed to put up a notice saying that they were supported by voluntary contribution and in 1873 there were six well women but they ceased to be appointed after 1875. [43]

MARTHA NORTON,
Aged 88
Upwards of FIFTY YEARS the attendant at the Buxton Well
Herself a proof of its salubrious Spring.

Amusements in Plenty

The well-known writer on Derbyshire, Edward Bradbury, styled himself 'Strephon' after that 'Arcadian Shepherd' of Gilbert and Sullivan who turned out to be politically less rustic than first thought! This allowed Bradbury to comment widely on the delights of nature and the social milieu and manners in his beloved High Peak. In 1891 he described a Buxton of one hundred years before giving us a lively picture of life in the Georgian Spa:

'...The best London talent appeared at the Theatre, for the metropolitan play-houses were closed during the Buxton season. The performances commenced at six o'clock, the latest hour for table d'hote being four o'clock. The Assembly Room was the scene of aristocratic dances The White Hart sent its respectful complimants to the Angel, and asked its company to their dance after supper. Other inns exchanged mutual courtesies of this description. There were no bath-chairs. It was the age of sedan-chairs. Oil lamps in the streets made the darkness visible. Link-men with flaring torches were the escort of ball-parties. The Assembly Room...was a blaze of wax candles in crystal chandeliers...the sedan-chairs set down radient beauties with powdered hair and jewelled dresses; chaperones and dowagers, fine old "bucks" and gallant beaux with marvellous wigs, coats of Tyrian bloom, bravely embriodered waistcoats, and garter-blue-silk breeches and dangling swords. The windows sent yellow shafts of light across the roadway. Music floats in the night-air...' [44]

A busy Georgian Crescent [by R. Grundy Heape]

CHAPTER THREE

Early 19th Century

Between 1803 and 1806 the architects, John White and Son, drew plans for improvements at Buxton which were, in part, intended to tidy up the area around the Crescent. The plans included the Square, designed as a group of lodging houses, and a new layout to the rear of the Crescent as well as the new St John's Church. The overall site plan, drawn by J. White jnr. in 1803 and modified in 1806, showed the proposed new developments and a number of existing buildings including the Baths.[1]

The evidence from John Carr's building accounts, set out in the last chapter, leads us to conclude that the White plan shows the layout of the baths existing in 1806 but does not show any proposed new baths since a total of seven baths are shown which, despite some small differences in orientation, almost exactly fit the description given by Denman in 1793.[2]

Two further pieces of evidence support this, firstly, examination of the original plan shows that the proposed new developments eg. the Square, St John's Church, are edged in red but the baths are not so edged. Secondly, and more importantly, the Devonshire Buxton Estate accounts for 1806 show the, comparatively, large sum of £1273 for a new bath and alteration of others, but these changes do not appear on the plan.[3] We can be fairly certain, therefore, that the main work carried out to the baths under John White and Son was the provision of a new Gentlemen's Bath and dressing rooms, some minor renovation to others and the filling in of the Cold Bath by the river. The site of this Cold Bath was used to build a new billiard room in 1810, also designed by John White.[4]

Jewitt, who published his *History of Buxton* in 1811, confirms these changes in his description of the baths as follows:

'...*The Baths lie to the west of St Anne's Well, and are seven in number, viz. = one public and two private for gentlemen; one public and one private for ladies; one, in which the water may be made to imitate that of Matlock; and one for the indiscriminate use of the poor. All except the Charity Bath have dressing rooms attached to them, furnished with every thing necessary or convenient for bathers, and servants to assist them in and out of the water...*'[5]

The additional gentlemen's bath by John White and Son, was called the 'new' bath and was situated to the rear of the Gentlemen's Private Bath. Dr Charles Scudamore, writing in 1820, refers to the gentlemen's 'new' bath which is likely to be this same bath since the estate accounts between 1806 and 1820 show an average yearly maintenance outlay of just over £100 but no further large expenditure.[6] It would not be unusual for the term 'new' to be applied to a bath for some years. Further confirmation is provided by Dr Carstairs writing in 1847 who referred to this bath having been built '...*about forty years ago...*'.[7] In addition to the White's plan of 1803/6 there exists a plan entitled 'Old Plan of Baths Approaches and the Square as existing prior to the alterations about 1851' which a number of writers have assumed to have been drawn in about 1851. Careful examination of this plan, however, suggests that it may have been drawn up by the Whites, certainly the style of drawing is very similar and it offers an update of the 1803/6 plan with the term 'new' applied not only to the Gentlemen's Private Bath but also to dressing rooms and the billiard room. In effect, it shows the White modifications to the Natural Baths and it could be of a much earlier date than 1851.[8]

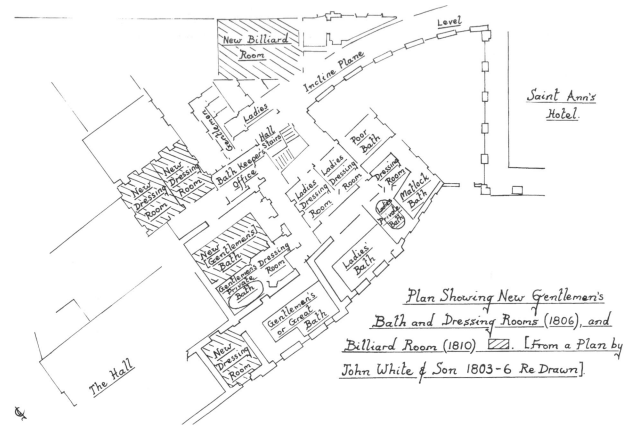

Plan showing new Gentlemen's Bath and dressing rooms (1806) and billiard room (1810) by John White & Son.

The Devonshire Estate took a healthy clear profit from the Natural Baths in the years between 1811 and 1820 of about £1000 per year. The year of Napoleon's defeat at the battle of Waterloo, 1815, showed particularly good profit at £1202.

The Buxton Spa drew members of the aristocracy and titled persons and, increasingly in the 19th century the wealthy middle-class trades-people, mill owners, cotton factors, manufacturers and others in a substantial way of business. Such people, coming to take the waters, would bring their family and, possibly, meet up with friends in town, so entertainment and diversions were required. Bott's new guide of 1795 referred in the title to '...*that place of health and amusement...*' and he described Buxton as '...*a place of resort for pleasure, as well as for health; the common amusements are, in the morning, taking the air, and sometimes hunting, in the evening, plays and dancing...*' adding a necessary description of the kind of culinary delights the visitor might expect:

> '...*Buxton is well supplied with fish from Warrington, Manchester and Sheffield during the season; there are fine trout and craw fish in the river Wye, which rises near Buxton, but the finest of the former are to be found in the Latkhill and Bradford about ten or twelve miles from Buxton. The town is well supplied with beef, veal, mutton, lamb, vegetables and fruit during the season...*' [9]

The Assembly Room in the Crescent had been designed by John Carr to provide just this kind of entertainment, assemblies for dancing and cards with coffee rooms close by all regulated by a Master of Ceremonies and a subscription book to record names and payment of those attending. Rules of entry, dress and conduct were designed to keep the Assembly Room 'exclusive' though in practice the ability to pay the seasonal admission of one guinea per person acted as the ultimate filter and the burgeoning 'nouveaux riches' were able to mix with the old aristocracy at Buxton. Hutchinson's guide describes the Assembly Rooms and some of the other attractions:

'...Buxton can also boast of a grand assembly room. The dress balls are on Wednesdays - the undress on Mondays and Fridays. There is a theatre, and generally a tolerable company of comedians... There are also billiard rooms innumerable, a news room at the Great Hotel as well as Mr Moore's room for the same purpose, and two circulating libraries. The petrifaction shops, where the Derbyshire spa is worked into chimney and other ornaments, may be seen in all directions...' [10]

Engraving showing how Hall Bank would have looked in the 1830s.
The lodging houses run down from top left of the image

A letter written by a young lady to her sister in 1810 gives a very evocative picture of life in Buxton for the visitor at that time:

'...Hall Bank, Buxton, August 19th 1810.

Dear sister,

To convince you that your desires have always with me the force of commands, I send you this journal of the manner in which I have passed my time since my arrival in this romantic village. You recollect that it was on Thursday, the 9th instant that my uncle and my aunt, my brother and myself , left home. As I am under no promise to give the particulars of our journey, I shall only say that we arrived here on the Saturday following, without having experienced any inconveniences but what naturally arise from travelling; except that before the conclusion of our ride, my aunt began to complain of more than the ordinary rheumatic pains in her arms and shoulders, and my uncle to be more than usually attentive to his feet and ancles.

We spent the remainder of the day of our arrival as most travellers in our situation would have done, or as most of the visitors of Buxton do, that is, we took possession of our apartments, made tea, sent for one of the resident physicians to consult him on the case of my uncle and aunt, enquired what families were then in the village, lolled an hour or two at the window, took an early supper, and went to bed.

SUNDAY. My brother and I rose at six, and drank each a glass of water at St Anne's Well. (Bye the bye, I cannot help remarking, that the drinking room is uncommonly neat, and uncommonly small. Charles, who you know last summer visited Bath and Cheltenham, finds fault with it, and says that if it had been extended along the front of the Crescent, where the posts and chains are, and provided with recesses and benches for the repose and accommodation "des buveurs", it would have been far more commodious, as it then would have afforded a facility of forming acquaintance, and have offered an excellent retreat from a rainy morning.) Walked across the gravel, I think they call it, (the Crescent Parade would certainly have been a better name,) round St Anne's Cliffe, and so to our apartments. I have heard you speak highly of St Anne's Cliffe, and indeed I coincide with you in sentiment. It is a pleasant walk, and the many glimpses (I cannot call them views) it affords of the Crescent renders it very interesting.

On entering our lodgings, my uncle and aunt were just setting out to bathe. I accompanied my aunt, and Charles his uncle. I think I never enjoyed so greater pleasure as bathing. The ladies' private bath is very convenient; but I need not describe it: you know it very well, and if you did not, as you only want an account of my time, it would not fall in with the plan prescribed. After breakfast, that is at eleven o'clock, we went to hear divine service in the Assembly Room, which I find is fitted up in a temporary manner as a chapel every Sunday throughout the season. Perhaps before the expiration of another, the church which his Grace of Devonshire is building may be completed. It is a fine building, and will be worthy to rank with the Crescent. At dinner, as newcomers, we entered our names in the subscription book for the Charitable Institution. I think it is wrong not to permit those who are so inclined to give more than a shilling to the fund, since by a small increase in the subscription, the allowance to the poor objects who are recommended to the waters, might be augmented. At present they receive but six shillings a week, which I cannot help thinking very inadequate to their support. In the evening we took a turn along the new walks; these in a few years will form an enchanting promenade, but the trees at present are too young to afford either shade or shelter. I am informed that this was a few years ago a piece of boggy ground, in which, on digging drains, the trunks of many trees were found entire, which by their colour appear to have been buried for ages. They were quite black, but notwithstanding very sound, and much resembled unwrought ebony in appearance. My uncle says, that naked as this country is now, it was once covered with wood, and that in all probability this tract made part of Peak forest. The walks are well laid out; and the cascade, the work of last winter, has a very pretty effect. Charles says they would yet bear much improvement; and that if the plantations and walks were carried forward to an old clump of firs, which appears at a little distance in the uninclosed and uncultivated marsh, and the water on this side left to spread out as its natural situation invites it to do, into a lake that might easily be made to empty its superfluous waters into the streams below, by a cascade similar to that already made, it would add much to the beauty of the whole, and form a more extended walk. For my part, I do not understand these kind of improvements, but as he pointed them out to me with his cane, I could not but coincide with his opinion, and admire his taste.

After supper, two ladies and gentlemen, who have apartments in the same house with us, my brother and myself, made a party for an excursion to Castleton on the following morning; and accordingly on MONDAY, about six o'clock, we set out. We spent upwards of an hour at the Ebbing and Flowing Well, which you remember is close to the road about five miles from Buxton, and saw the water rise and fall twice. We all felt hurt to find so great a curiosity in so uncleanly and neglected a state; and it gave us no high opinion of the taste of the proprietor of the land, who could suffer such a singular spring to remain uninclosed by a building which should prevent it from being polluted and disturbed by cattle...

Peveril Castle at Castleton

We arrived at Castleton at about ten, having made a short deviation from our road to take a peep at Elden Hole, for you see I am not willing to let anything curious escape me; saw the Speedwell Mine, Mam Tor, Peak's Hole, and the Castle; went forward to Bradwell, spent half an hour in Bagshaw's Cavern, and returned by Tideswell. As you saw these places two years ago, I need not trouble you with any description of them. At eight o'clock the whole party went to the assembly. We found it better attended by ladies than gentlemen, for this being the 12th of August, the day of opening the moors, as it is called, all the younger part of the male visitors had been out grouse-shooting, and were in general too fatigued to engage in a dance at their return.

TUESDAY. We (I mean the same party as yesterday) visited Poole's-Hole in the forenoon, and took a ramble among the lime houses. What wretched habitations are these for beings of the human kind! And yet for these artificial caves, which, in all conscience, are dear enough at the making, the inhabitants pay a yearly rent to the Lord of the Manor. In the afternoon, the weather being wet, we spent an hour in walking along the arcade; this is a very convenient promenade for bad weather. We then called at Mr Moore's, entered our names as subscribers to his excellent library, brought each of us a book, and spent the remainder of the afternoon in reading. Garnett's Tour into Scotland was the work which I chose for my amusement, a work which I should not have expected to find in any subscription library; but Mr Moore's contains in general only stirling works. I forgot to say that my brother and the gentleman, instead of favouring us with their company at our books, adjourned to the billiard-room. After tea, we visited the theatre. What a mean building! but for the words Pit and Boxes over the door, it would be mistaken for a barn. We found it much prettier within: it was newly painted,

Miners Cottage, near Buxton.

Lime houses in Grin Woods

Waterfall at Lovers Leap Buxton

Lovers' Leap near Duke's Drive.

and the performers were better than we could have expected on such a stage; some indeed were excellent in their line.

WEDNESDAY, The morning was very unfavourable, I therefore employed myself in admiring the charming views which embellish the "Tour" I mentioned. After dinner, the same party continuing, we took a walk to the Lover's Leap, (I think there is a Lover's Leap in every mountainous country), and turning up the dell at the corner of that rock, were agreeably surprised by one of the most beautiful cascades imaginable. Perhaps it might be owing to the heavy and continued rains, which fell the day and night before, that it appeared so interesting; for I think I have heard you mention examining this dell, without noticing any waterfall. On enquiry, I find that it is formed by a winter stream, and, that at any other season it is never observable but after heavy rains. You know my turn for botany: this dell, and the adjoining rocks afforded me a high treat; and though my "compagnons de voyage" did not understand that science, they assiduously assisted me in procuring a number of plants which I have hitherto considered as rare. I have preserved many specimins with which I hope to amuse you on my return home. This evening being a dress-ball, and Buxton having within these few days had a number of arrivals of the first fashion, the Assembly Room appeared to me uncommonly brilliant.

THURSDAY, In the forenoon made a family party to a concert; in the afternoon took an airing on horseback round the ride; and in the evening, attended the theatre.

FRIDAY, The morning part of Friday, was employed by me, my brother, and the remainder of our party, in visiting Chee-Tor, and Miller's-Dale. I never more regretted my inability to take an accurate sketch, than on viewing this charming vale. Everything that can render a picture interesting, may be found here, and all combine to produce a lovely landscape. Charles has finished a view of it from below the lower mill, which I am sure will afford you some amusement. On the other side of a hill, near the upper mill, we picked up many specimins of the Derbyshire diamond. After rain they lie sparkling in the road. As you never mentioned these things to me, it is probable you never saw them: you will, I hope, have that pleasure on my return. In the afternoon, the weather continuing extremely fine, we took a walk to the top of Axe-edge. This mountain, by its height, commands several extensive prospects, and produces many plants which cannot be cultivated in low situations. I found one or two cloud-berries near its summit. I need not, I think, tell you that we were too much fatigued with our walk, to be able to attend the assembly. A good night's rest completely restored us, and yesterday morning, SATURDAY, the 18th, we set out, about six o'clock, in three chaises, to look at Chatsworth. The house is noble, the situation fine, the country grand and picturesque, but the water-works are very inferior. We returned through Hassop, a beautiful village belonging to F. Eyre Esq. Great and Little Longstone, and along the edge of Monsal-Dale. I know not, my dear sister, whether you have, or have not seen this enchanting spot; but surely so many beauties as are to be found in this lovely vale, are not often assembled together. I know not how to describe it, so can only recommend to you to visit it on your next coming to Buxton. About six o'clock in the evening, we arrived again at Buxton, well satisfied with our journey, and concluded the day with another visit to the theatre. Thus, my dear sister, you may perceive that the first week of my residence in Buxton, has been passed in a round of ever-varying amusement; and from the many interesting antiquities, scenes, and curiosities, in the neighbourhood, which yet remain to be examined, I am confident that a longer stay than mine may be passed, not only without the ennui too frequently attendant on public places, but with the greatest entertainment and delight. We purpose in the course of this week to visit Dove-Dale, an excursion, which, in all probability, will find employment for two days. We also intend visiting the Diamond-hill; and that long neglected curiosity, the Marvel-Stones, which, though almost unknown to the inhabitants of Buxton, lies within five miles of this village. I am informed that Mr Bray has described them in his tour published about 30 years ago. My uncle and aunt who are now almost without ailment, propose to join our excursional party next week, and the week after we intend to be in Matlock, from which place, if I find anything worth communicating, I may possibly date my next letter; till when,

I remain, Dear Sister, Your ever affectionate, E.S... [11]

The young lady 'E.S.' is a fine example of the 'romantic' of her day, interested in scenery, wildlife, flora and fauna, though in all her many excursions she does not have the time, or perhaps, inclination to describe the course of treatment her aunt and uncle were experiencing, except to say that they are much better after the first week.

The Earliest Hot Baths

In chapter two we have seen that attempts were made to artificially raise the temperature of the Gentlemen's Private Bath by the use of flues. It would seem, however, that the purpose of this was merely to raise the temperature of a colder bath to one which more closely approximated the natural mineral water temperature of 82°F (27.5°C). Whilst describing these arrangements in 1801 Denman had also strongly advocated the provision of baths which could be heated to 'precise' temperatures for the treatment of such complaints as calcifications, bowel inflammation and kidney disorder. This medical recommendation must have gathered momentum and the Devonshire Estate took the decision to expand the

The flat roof of the Hot Baths of 1818, designed by Charles Sylvester, are to the right.

facilities by the erection of Hot Baths in about 1816. Payments to carpenters, stone masons and plumbers working on the baths first appear in the 1817 accounts and by 20th May 1818 the baths were open for business. In that year the Estate took a clear profit of just under £250.

The baths were designed by Charles Sylvester of Derby, who was something of a specialist in the installation of hot baths equipment. He was paid £86.18s.0d [£86.90] for drawings and his attendance during the erection and £32 for a warm air stove. The baths were lined with white marble and Dutch tiles, the tiles purchased from the Staffordshire firm of Josiah Wedgwood, and the total building cost was just over £1630. In 1819 the Devonshire Estate paid £615 for an additional bath with a further sum of £104 for the completion of the hot baths and in 1820 Charles Sylvester was paid £41.8s [£41.40p] for superintending the building of the additional bath which included fitting apparatus for raising the temperature of the water. The Hot Baths were fed from the overflow of the St Anne's Well and it is likely that this was supplemented with water from the Bingham spring situated at the east end of the Crescent.[12]

These Hot Baths were situated at the east end of the Crescent and had direct access from the Great hotel with a public access from a door opposite the Grove hotel. At this time the Crescent was enclosed by a high stone wall with an entrance through an iron gate opposite the Grove hotel, this area being known as 'Irongate'. The Hot Baths curved round from this point to join the Crescent but the building, which had a flat, lead covered, roof was masked by trees and in some contemporary engravings it is not shown. An old Buxtonian recalls passing by the 'blank walls' of the Hot Baths and the general opinion of writers in the 1820s was that the Hot Baths building was unpretentious but that inside it was very well equipped with shower baths, spray pumps and dressing boxes.[13]

The Natural Baths in 1820

The development of the Hot Baths, as an important additional provision, caused some changes to the Natural Baths facilities for by 1820 the Matlock Bath was no longer provided. It is possible that medical fashion had changed causing a decline in its use for treatments but a more likely reason is that it was no longer needed. By now the new Hot Baths could offer a varying degree of temperature control and the Tonic, or cold plunging, bath was available on Macclesfield road. (This Tonic bath was, in fact, likened to a Matlock Bath by some medical practitioners). Further work on the Natural Baths took place in the years 1821/22 and a detailed examination of the accounts leads us to suggest that, in addition to the installation of ventilation stoves in the Baths building, the Matlock Bath structure was brought back into use to provide a Charity Bath for ladies. Evidence for this is that expenditure was considerably higher in those two years than in any subsequent year up to 1833 when we know there were two separate baths for male and female charity patients each measuring ten foot eight inches long by ten foot wide and by four foot eight inches deep. The only other significant expenditure was in 1825/6 when the baths were relined with porcelain tiles supplied by Josiah Wedgwood. From 1820 to 1840 the Natural Baths returned a clear profit of about £800 p.a. and, apart from the work described above, the Devonshire Buxton estate spent an average of £90 yearly on maintenance. A plan of the baths and Crescent area dating to about 1820 shows the extensive water management arrangements required for the provision of the Natural Baths suite. Each bath had to be fed and drained and a large sough (water channel) ran right round the outer curve of the Crescent to drain into the river at the east end. It is clear also, from an engraving of about the same time, that the external facade had been tidied up sometime between 1805 and 1820, possibly as part of the John White & Son work. The engraving shows the building housing the Great Bath and other gentlemen's baths having four storeys and its roof line raised to the same level as the Hall. The other baths are housed in a neat two bay, two story building adjacent.[14]

Resorting to Buxton

By the mid-1820s Buxton could rival any of the many spas in England of the time with its full range of Baths, resident and visiting doctors, and associated medical treatments but it was still necessary to enhance the social amenities available. The thirty years to 1850 were challenging for an inland resort such as Buxton. Wealthy manufacturers were deterred from leaving their works by the unrest amongst

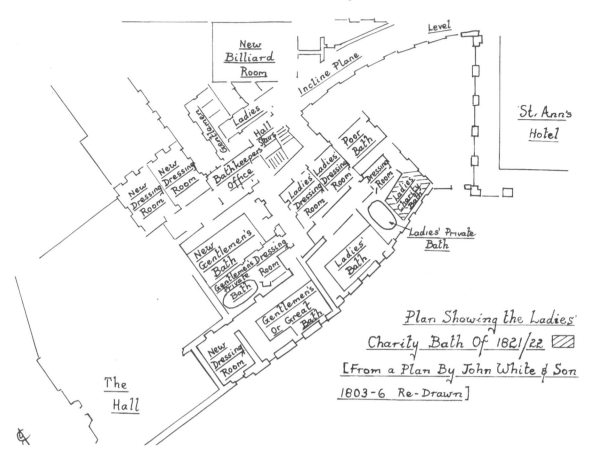

Plan showing the Ladies' Charity Bath (1821-22)

Engraving showing the Natural Baths by 1820.
They are seen as the low two-storey building between the Hall Hotel (left) and the Crescent (right)

the working class through the Chartist movement, strong in the manufacturing towns around Stockport and Manchester. This was exacerbated by harsh winters leading to high unemployment and poor harvests such as those of 1828 and 1829 which fuelled unrest. There was challenge too from the seaside resorts who were vying with the spas for holiday business, resorts such as Southport and Lytham were in strong competition with Buxton and Harrogate. Competition too, after the French wars, came from the continent where the spas were again opened to the English traveller. Spas such as the French Vichy, the Bavarian resorts of Kissingen and Sulzbad, Pyrmont and Wildbad also in Germany, and the Czech spa of Karlsbad, known today as Karlovy Vary.

The competition was perceived to be strong enough for Dr W.H. Robertson to remark in his first book, in 1838, that the waters on the Continent were generally inferior to that of Buxton.[15] The hotels in the Crescent were part of the Duke of Devonshire's Buxton Estate and when the St Anne's, the Centre, the Great and the Hall Hotels built up considerable arrears of rent, the duke's agent, Phillip Heacock, did much to ease the position of the proprietors. He also worked tirelessly to promote Buxton, he had obtained the market charter in 1813 and, after his success in installing new Hot Baths, he had soft spring water brought from a spring in Manchester Road to serve the hotels and lodging houses in the Crescent and the Square.

The Duke of Devonshire's architect Jeffry Wyatt was commissioned in 1818 to lay out the slopes in front of the Crescent and baths as a series of graduated terraced walks. In 1828 a new, modest promenade and music room was constructed in the Crescent and in 1833 a new theatre was built opposite the Hall Hotel. The Devonshire Estate also provided the public band, described as an excellent band of musicians, which played in the Crescent, Hall Gardens, Promenade and Assembly Rooms.[16]

Daniel Orme's *Buxton Guide* of 1823 described the entertainments thus:

'...The chief amusements are hunting, shooting, fishing, plays, assemblies, riding and walking; and there are many public tables, to which strangers may resort and meet with the first company. This is the more pleasing, as sociability appears to be the great aim of the visitors of this truly fashionable and beneficial watering-place. The town contains lodging houses for the accommodation of all ranks in society, and shops of every description... Messrs. Brights, the Jewellers under the Piazzas in the Square, have always a most elegant display of valuable and fashionable Jewellery, Cutlery, Plate and Plated Goods, Piano Fortes for hire by the week or month, Music, and other articles; and their shop is the resort of all the fashionable company who visit Buxton... There are many shops which display the most beautiful articles of spa manufacture, minerals, fossils, and a variety of curious specimins of nature and art, peculiar to Derbyshire; particularly a beautiful spa, denominated Blue John, formerly used in repairing the roads, but now manufactured into the most elegant vases &c. and purchased at the great expence of forty guineas a ton...'[17]

The attractions around Buxton were enthusiastically described in the guide books, Poole's Hole, the Dukes's Drive, and Lover's Leap close by and, a little further afield, Chee Tor, the ebbing and flowing well at Barmoor Clough, the marvel stones, the Mam Tor shimmering mountain, Peveril Castle and Peak Cavern with the other caverns in Castleton. Many of these had been known to visitors since the 17th century and continued to attract the tourist throughout the 19th century as, indeed, some still do today. The noted wood engraver, Thomas Bewick (1753-1828) stayed in lodgings at Hall Bank when he was advised to take the waters for gout in his stomach in June of 1827. He visited Poole's Hole but did not enter the cave and on another day his friend, John Dovaston, engaged a vehicle and driver to take Bewick, his two daughters Jane and Isabella and himself via Fairfield and Mam Tor to Castleton. There they inspected Peak

Portrait of Thomas Bewick (1753-1828)
the noted wood engraver

Cavern, whose description - *'the Devil's Arse i' the Peak'* - intrigued him, before enjoying a picnic in Peveril Castle. Bewick, whose *History of British Birds* was very successful, took a natural interest in the flora, noting the fern and lichens and collecting nettle-tops to boil for soup; but he was particularly keen to see a ring ouzel and was delighted when a pair landed amongst gilly-flowers on a wall at the castle.[18]

In August of 1824 Anne Lister visited Buxton for seven weeks with her aunt who was taking water treatment for rheumatism. They stayed, with two servants, at the Great Hotel and she filled her time supervising her aunt's treatment, walking around the town, reading local guide books and other literature from the subscription library, corresponding with her intimate friends, and driving out in a gig to places around Buxton which included a day trip to Bakewell. Anne Lister's aunt was treated by the local apothecary, Peter Flint and by Sir Charles Scudamore, who visited in the season.

Her diary entry, Friday 5 August, records the first consultation: *'...Sat on the sofa talking to my aunt till 8, having sent for Mr Flint, the apothecary. He came and staid perhaps 10 minutes or 1/4 hour. A very vulgar man but my aunt was pleased we had sent for him & we hope he wil do her good. He had just sent her an aperient draught & will order about her bath tomorrow. She is not to stay [in] more than six minutes... Said I intended to bathe. How long should I stay in, who was not an invalid? 1/4 hour. On saying I had been used to stay an hour, he wondered that I should have tried my constitution so much. Did it not weaken me very much? I might drink the waters, only should take care of the state of my bowels...'*

She also gives a good description of the food at the Great Hotel describing the dinner of mock turtle soup, trout, mutton, and saddle, leg and loin of lamb roasted together as good and excellent.[19]

Spring by Thomas Bewick

Chalybeate Spring

Dr Denman, in the second edition of his book (1801) noted that the chalybeate spring situated near the George Inn was still contaminated, muddy and unfit for use, despite the fact that it was protected by a small dome or arch. It was still out of use in 1811 when Jewitt observed that the water *'...preserved in a gritstone basin arched over...'* had become shamefully neglected and was totally unfit for use. This suggests that the water was unavailable for at least 30 years. In 1819, however the well was rebuilt at a cost of

£9.18s.1d. and it was in use again, from that time being maintained by the Devonshire Buxton Estate.

It is likely that this rebuilding included routing the water through a sculpted lion's mouth, guide books from 1820 show engravings of this 'lion's mouth' well and Dr Robertson, writing in 1838, said that the chalybeate was commonly referred to in the town as 'lion's mouth water'.[20] As an iron bearing water it was considered weak but very pure, its temperature was 54° F. (12.1° C.) It was considered by Dr Robertson as a useful tonic for the eyes but also effective for 'indolent swelling' of the joints when poured from a spouted jug over the affected joints two or three times a day.

The medical practitioner, T.J. Page, who was surgeon to the Buxton Bath Charity in the 1840s, cites the successful use of the chalybeate in the case of a young lady with 'gastrodynia' (pain in the stomach). He prescribed two half pints to be taken each day and said that, within a fortnight, she was well and had no return of the ailment.[21] So here we see examples of the chalybeate water being prescribed as both an internal and external treatment. After 1845 the chalybeate well in George Street was covered with an 'umbrella like' structure which was removed in 1858 and placed in the Crescent to provide a cover for for the town band.[22] By 1853 water from the chalybeate well had been piped into a new well room provided as part of the newly designed Natural Baths building.

The chalybeate spring or
'Lion's Mouth Well'

Chalybeate Spring.

The Early Victorian Natural Baths

The provision in the Natural Baths remained largely the same from the mid 1820s to the major rebuilding in the early 1850s. Writing in 1838, Dr WH Robertson, who was to become Buxton's best known medical specialist, described the Natural Baths as follows:

> *'...The natural baths, exclusive of those devoted to the use of the patients of the Buxton Bath Charity are five in number, respectively called "The Ladies' Public Bath" - "The Ladies' Private Bath" - "The Gentlemen's Public Bath" - "The Gentlemen's Large Private Bath" - and "The Gentlemen's Small Private Bath". Of these the oldest is the Gentlemen's Public Bath. It is lined with smooth stone. Through interstitial crevices, purposely left between the stones which form the floor of this bath, the water enters from the spring itself. The water in this bath is four feet*

nine inches deep. The length of the bath is rather more than 25 feet, and it is about 12½ feet wide. The temperature of the water in the bath is within a small fraction of 82 degrees by Fahrenheit's thermometer.

From this bath, at its south western-corner, a portion of the water, as it comes through the natural crevices of the limestone, is cut off and collected in a reservoir, from which three of the other baths are supplied by pipes, which are laid with such jealous care, that the water only loses one degree of heat in its passage from the reservoir to any of the baths suppled from it. The Gentlemen's small private bath is of an oval shape. The long diameter of it is 13½ feet, the short diameter 6 feet. The temperature of the water in this bath is within a fraction of 81½ degrees. The bath is lined with white porcelain. The Gentlemen's large private bath is of an oblong square shape. Its length is 21 feet, its breadth more than 10½ feet. The bath is lined with white porcelain. The depth of the water in this bath and in the Gentlemen's small private bath is 4 feet 8 inches. The Ladies' public bath is an oblong square. Its length is 21 feet, its breadth 12 feet. The depth of water in the bath is 4 feet 6 inches. It is lined with smooth stone. The Ladies' private bath is 12 feet long, and 4½ feet wide. The depth of water is 4 feet 6 inches. It is lined with white porcelain. All these baths are provided with forcing-pumps, by which the water may be directed against any affected part with very considerable force. Proper dressing rooms, well aired, are attached to the several baths; towels, bathing gowns etc., are of course provided; servants are in constant attendance to supply every requisite assistance; screens and waterproof dresses are provided to enable any part to be pumped upon without rendering it necessary to immerse the rest of the body; a convenient machine is in readiness to lower the extremely infirm into the water; and, in short, no means are left untried, to deprive the bathers of Buxton of what has been said to be necessary to Englishmen - a something of which to complain , and at which to grumble.' [23]

These five baths for paying patients and the two Charity Baths were unchanged when described by Dr Carstairs in 1847. He referred to the Gentlemen's Private bath as the 'Duke's Bath' and the Gentlemen's Large Private bath (still being described in 1839 as the 'New Bath') as the 'Gentlemen's Two Shilling Bath'. He also described the Charity Baths, one for men and one for women, as being in a yard adjoining the Ladies Bath. The yard referred to was an open space between the baths and the Crescent through which access to the Charity Baths was gained.

The water for drinking was dispensed from St Anne's Well, the Grecian style building, designed by Carr and situated in the Crescent, opposite the Natural Baths. Dr Robertson observed that the effects of the Buxton waters, when taken internally, were in some degree the same as those produced when used as a bath. He set out the regime for taking the water as follows:

'...Half a pint is the quantity commonly taken at once. It is usual to take the first dose before breakfast and the remainder during the forenoon. It is justly considered to be most improper to drink the waters shortly before going into the bath.... It is seldom necessary to take more than a pint and a half of these waters every day but cases do occasionally occur in which it is found to be by no means wise to restrict the patient to the use of this quantity of the waters, but in which considerably more, and probably twice this quantity, is taken with advantage...' [24]

Victorian Water Treatments

The bathing treatments advocated by Dr Scudamore in the late 1830s, centred around immersion in the baths for specific periods of time and the use of pumps to spray affected parts of the body with varying degrees of force. Scudamore suggested that patients resorting to Buxton were suffering, usually but not exclusively, from gout or rheumatism and he advocated medication and other forms of treatment in conjunction with the water regime. A recent medical thesis has summarised the types of treatment prescribed by Scudamore from an extensive number of case histories in his book published in 1839:

'...For rheumatism and gout it was recommended that an antiphologistic (poultice) be applied before bathing and, for stubborn attacks, a technique of blistering was used to increase the blood supply to the specific area and to concentrate the body's own curative powers. The blister was formed by applying a caustic substance and the cuticle was removed on vestication (ie. the superficial skin was removed after the blister had formed) when two grains of acetate of morphia (highly soluble) were then rubbed into the cutis (the underlying skin). This, not surprisingly, led to 48 pain free hours. Leeches were also applied to local areas of inflammation then warm water pumped over the area followed by shampooing (massage). Medication in the form of colchicum (a garden bulb which was used until recently in the treatment of gout) or quinine was used to reduce fever. Quinine was also used for neuralgia and morphine was given for pain relief. If the patient did not return to full vigour a tonic, in the form of liquor arsenalis might be offered, as Sir Charles Scudamore said "...in particular forms of disease we can avail ourselves of this powerful mineral tonic without fear of injury. Yet I must observe it is not a medicine to be given on common occasions nor ever without a careful watching of its effects..." Arsenic was also used in skin complaints and sasparilla doubled as a treatment for both chronic rheumatism and skin disease.

Sciatica was treated by having mercury rubbed into the affected part to the extent of causing ptyalism (meaning excessive salivation, a symptom of early mercury poisoning). Mercury was chiefly used to treat syphillis. Carbonate of iron (a tonic) was taken by day and as much 'black drop' with acetate of morphia and camphor as necessary for sleep and tranquility at night. Black drop is presumed to be liquorice water (though tar water was also used as a curative from the 18th century).

Stomach and liver troubles were treated with bark saline in effervescence with free doses of the black drop or Brandish's alkaline (probably a local apothecary) and disulphate of quinine. Infections of the respiratory tract were dealt with by application of acetate of conium liniment to sedate the respiratory centre and having analgesic properties to soothe any pain (this treatment is a compound of Hemlock which causes death by asphyxiation). Liniments were also used on painful joints, namely, soap liniment, belladonna (which is poisonous if applied to broken skin) and veratia which had analgesic properties...'[25]

This shows the range of medication becoming available in the early 19th century. Dr Scudamore used these treatments in conjunction with various forms of water bathing, douche and massage. He advised that the baths should be emptied and refilled every day and that the utmost cleanliness should be observed in all the bathing arrangements. The Buxton surgeon T.J. Page offered five rules of bathing:

> *'...First go into the Bath about the middle of the day.*
> *Second - to go into the Bath when the body is warm*
> *Third - to go in with the feet first*
> *Fourth - to remain in the water FIRST but a very short time*
> *Fifth - To bathe on alternate days, or to miss every third day...'* [26]

Vapour bath at Buxton

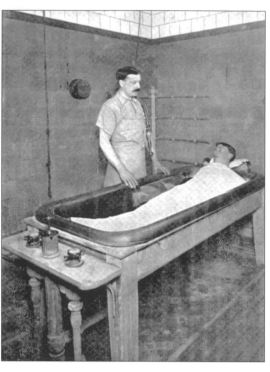

Buxton massage & douche

Hot Bath with crane

Hot Bath with douche

The term 'Public' and 'Private' is frequently used to describe baths and it may be helpful to explain the distinction. As far as we can ascertain a 'Private' bath would be used by a single patient at any one time whereas a 'Public' bath would be used by several patients together. As medical techniques developed beyond simple bathing and rudimentary massage and douche sprays, it was recognised that a large expanse of water was not required for single patient treatment and the size of 'Private' baths became smaller.

Diary of a Buxton Patient

Mrs Mary Eizabeth Cruso of Leek, who came to take the water treatment in 1836 gives a day-by-day account of life for the patient in her diary, describing both her medical and social experiences. She is, at one point, non too complimentary about Dr Scudamore who together with Dr Thomas Buxton of Market Place and Dr Thomas Drever (1768-1849) attended her. She refers to Dr Drever as Driver. She also received the medical attention of Mrs Ainley who was a medical rubber, or shampooer (ie masseuse) from Sheffield and had been coming to Buxton in the season since 1826.

Mrs Mary Cruso was 41 years old and suffered from gout, which may have been an hereditary complaint, she also suffered from rheumatism. Her doctor in Leek, Mr Charles Flint advised her to visit Buxton after several months of unsuccessful treatment with leeches, poultices of camomile flowers, cooling powders, fomentations, and colchicum.

Thus it was that, on Monday the 27th of June 1836, Mrs Mary Elizabeth Cruso and her servant Olive travelled to Buxton and took rooms in the St Ann's Hotel in the Crescent. During her stay she had a number of visitors including regular visits from her husband John, partner in a legal firm, and her brother Michael and his family made a visit. She also socialised with a number of other visitors to Buxton in the manner of a woman of her station:

.....25th JUNE
Michael [her brother] went to Buxton this morning to see after rooms for me at St Ann's, which he procured and engaged them for Monday therefore that job is fixed but I think I shall be obliged to go into lodgings room as I shall find the hotel too expensive. Mrs Michael very poorly with weaning.

27th JUNE
This morning rose rather earlier as I had to superintend Olive's packing and to be dressed and ready by twelve the hour the carriage is ordered. With a heavy heart I left my dear Husband and dear Home for Buxton. I had a pleasant ride and not so much fatigue as I expected - and now I am settled down dully enough to be sure at St Anne's Hotel. I have never stirred out of my sitting room as yet and I dread the ascending two pairs of stairs to my dormitory.

I have been seated at my window which looks into the Crescent gazing often in vacancy for few people are stirring and there seems but a slender allowance of visitors in this house - one Lady only besides myself and some gentlemen. Olive thinks she shall be tired and glad to see home again but it is rather too soon to be anticipating a return and after a nights rest and getting one's occupations together we shall both feel better.

28th JUNE
Got up this morning my pains and aches not charmed away. The band was playing in the Crescent when I went down. After Olive settled me on the sofa I fell into a painful reveries the melancholy airs, the lame

and the halt, the old and the young, without looks of animation or sounds of cheerfulness passing round and round the arcade appeared as if struck by the wand of an enchanter who had doomed them to perpetual motion in one spot. When the music ceased the enchantment was over and the noble cold looking Crescent was left to solitude and to me as I saw no one (but myself) at any of the windows. About one I was drawn in a bath chair to the bath. The afternoon and evening passed painfully and wearisome and would have been still duller had not Miss Crossland, who is staying at the Grove, sat with me for an hour or two.

Today I bought a new vehicle for being carried up and down stairs the price 2 guineas for I was in constant apprehension as they carried me in an armchair last night that I shou'd have found myself speedily at the bottom of the stairs again. Went to bed at 12.

29th JUNE

Two nights I have passed without sleeping draughts and both tolerably good ones. I feel achy and painful but they tell me Buxton must pain before it can cure. I have written a long full and particular account of myself to my Husband this morning. Staid in my own room until I had finished. Just as I had sealed my letter and was giving it to Olive to convey to the post office she entered with one from dear Johnny and a newspaper which young Barlow [son of the landlord of the Red Lion Inn, Leek] had brought from Leek. Amelia Crossland was with me and I had asked her to drink tea with me in the evening. At one was wheeled to my bath - no charms in the water this morning at least sensible ones for I can move no better coming out than going in. Got a new and agreeable book from the Library- one of James' called "One in a Thousand" - this whiled away my aching hours till Amelia came. We drank tea and a little after eight my dear hub made his appearance - anticipation and some fear that it might be in vain was lost in reality and I had him to myself affectionate and dear.

I think he seemed a little disappointed he did not see a little improvement in my movements which remain as clumsy and inelegant as rheumatism can make them. It really is bordering on the ridiculous to see the faces and distortions of most who pass my window. Were it not that suffering, (and no one who has not felt it can say what suffering), is the cause I could almost laugh for generally speaking the malady from which they suffer does not deprive the patient of rosy cheeks and plump appearance. John read to me till half past ten I then commenced my labours of accension and disrobing and it was twelve before I was ready to part with Olive.

30th JUNE

John left after breakfast and proceeded to Hopton he intends being at home tomorrow night and on Saturday I may see him again if nothing unforseen prevents his coming. When I came downstairs the band was again playing but I was feeling quite so melancholy and enjoyed it more unembittered by the very painful thoughts which presented themselves on Tuesday.

I spent most of the morning in writing to my sister but was too tired quite to finish my letter which I must do tomorrow. Amelia Crossland I only saw for a few minutes she being very poorly. In the evening, the Boots of St Anne's acted as my coachman and drew me in my bath chair out for an hour. Finished my amusing book and went rather earlier to bed having been obliged to give my Soutresse a slight reminder that I brought her to attend on me and not run about with other people's servants - she having left me for nearly two hours with open window etc, etc. A very fine warm day something like summer we have begun at home to cut our grass.

1st JULY

A true summer morning. I went to the bath at one and have actually walked three steps across the room tho' I feel much more pain in my thigh and leg and foot. After bathing, I felt a very uncomfortable pain in my groin from weakness and if it does not go off again before tomorrow I shall be obliged to delay bathing another day. It has increased all day and my little ride has not improved it. Amelia Crossland walked a short distance with me and introduced me to the Miss Woods and Miss Aston. It is strange I have met with no one I know since I came to this place.

2nd JULY

This morning I was obliged to give up my bath -I did not feel well enough and have had rather a bad night. I went out in the bath chair this evening; my morning was spent in reading and working. After being out for half an hour I saw my dear husband and Mr Cockburn [probably a colleauge of John Cruso] *an hour before their time, they got out and walked by my side until they thought it time I should go into the house.*

3rd JULY

John and Mr Cockburn went to church I came down about 12. I had a sleepless bad night and I have felt very poorly all day. I walked across the room with two last night but cannot today. In the evening the pain of gout came on and I really think I shall have an attack. If it will relieve my general system so much the better. Much to my sorrow I was obliged to part with my dear Hub and his companion again this evening they left about $^1/_2$ *past 8. Elizabeth the cook and Tom Bullock walked over to see Buxton and me this morning and returned at night.*

I had a nice ride this afternoon in the bath chair all round the plantation walk the Boots pulling my companions pushing when needful and I did not see Amelia today. Olive went to church at night.

4th JULY

Bathed this morning. I am quite helpless cannot move my foot for walking and have felt very poorly all day. Went out in the evening for an hour and retired an hour earlier to bed. Amelia I have seen for a few minutes only she being very poorly.

5th JULY

Was awoke early this morning with my sound foot giving symptom of intending to companionage my poor swollen one - A little creeping pain as if trying the ground for more acute attack round the nail and joint of my toe alarmed me but my hope of it leaving that foot and going to the other was soon over gradually it became more developed and the gout literally began in good earnest, on and on it crept till the sole and whole of my foot became affected and a painful day bid fair for a more painful night I did not bathe of course and now both feet being disabled prevented me crawling even to the bath chair had it been practicable to have put my foot in a comfortable position. Amelia Crossland called and I asked her to tea for tomorrow - I wrote to my Husband as I had promised, my foot keeping time to the music of the band and sent it by post - but to my astonishment in he came about $^1/_2$ *past 8. A good kind soul - he thought he left me very poorly on Sunday night and so came again the first moment he had but he is to go back by six tomorrow morning - Oh how I wish I cou'd always have him near me!*

6th JULY

A sleepless and very painful night but I am in hopes, this gout may relieve my system and therefore tho' I am suffering much I do not regret it. My other foot is rather less swollen I think and the pain in my thigh better. I did not get to sleep till quite morning and when I awoke found my dear one was gone and I had not kissed or said good bye to him. I quite thought of lying in bed all day and wish now I had done so but Olive was so sure that I shou'd be tired and I had some apprehension of it myself that with much difficulty and a good deal of pain was got up and dressed and carried down. I made them carry me from the chair to the sofa on the swing without the poles and find it a nice contrivance.

This morning as I was getting up Olive asked me if I knew Mrs Harrison of Snelson - No I do not - Why her maid told her that her Mistress had met me at Tissington (but she was mistaken) and said she was alone and shou'd be most happy if I wou'd take a ride with her in her carriage. Of course I felt obliged for her kindness and wrote a note to thank her but said the offer was made to one whom she thought she knew and I had never the pleasure of seeing her, tho' I was acquainted with Sir Henry and Lady Fitzherbert but shou'd be most happy to make her acquaintance if she wished for a little society during her visit here. She came to call upon me in the afternoon and so by accident I have made a most agreeable acquaintance for she seems a very pleasing agreeable woman and quite friendly and kind in her manners. Amelia came to tea and very ill I was all day, indeed towards night my pain became almost intolerable and I nearly fainted away from it. I took 16 drops of Colchicum three times during the day. As soon as possible I was got to bed but it seemed to abate as if the blood had taken a different direction and the pain in my thigh was better all day. I however again have determined not to get up again until I am better. The Band played 2 hours this evening.

7th JULY

My pain gradually going off I towards morning had some comfortable refreshing sleep and with a presentment that I was sure to have some visitors from Leek got up about 10. Whilst I was at breakfast, undressed as usual, we saw a pony carriage in which Olive declared was Mr & Mrs Michael, Henrietta and Polly [their daughters] and so it turned out as they soon made their appearance. My tears wou'd flow as I kissed them the gout must have something very lowering to the spirit I am sure tho' last night cried for pain. I was indeed glad to see them and also glad they did not come yesterday as I was much too poorly to have enjoyed their company. The band was playing when they came they therefore saw Buxton to perfection and Mary said she thought she cou'd stay a fortnight very well without being tired but before the day was over she began to think it was dullish. They went to Brights, [Jewellers & Fine Cutlers, in the Crescent] to see the baths, etc.

I felt better but not well by a great deal all day. We dined at ¹/₂ past four and to my surprise in walked Mr Flint. He thinks I have more feverish action and not looking so well - as Michael also told me -and that I was thinner. He gave me a prescription for the night draught and not much hope of being well very soon. He said if I was not better in a week or ten days to consult some one here as he did not like to give me medicine without he watch how it suited - he recommends me not to bathe until the inflammation is gone off on my foot.

8th JULY

Wrote to my dearest Father this morning I took one of Mr Flint's powders last night. Mrs Harrison sat with me a short time last evening and also called this morning and asked me if I was well enough to take a ride with her but I was obliged to decline as I cou'd not bother her with so many problems etc.. When I am more a little better I shall be glad to do so.

9th JULY

Got up rather better and had another good night. After lunch went out in the bath chair for a short time. Whilst at dinner the band played it remained for nearly an hour and half. Received a parcel from home but no note and I began to fear John was not coming as they said but about ½ past 8 he made his appearance much to my satisfaction. I have been looking after lodgings to day and this evening he went to see if they wou'd suit and has taken them for me I am to pay £1-1s.-0 d. for a drawing room 14s. for two bedrooms each. When he came back he told me the landlady seemed to know our birth parentage and education. [Mrs. Mary Boam who kept lodgings in The Square]

10th JULY

John went to church this morning I was downstairs when he returned. He then went to call on Mr & Mrs Harrison - he also called on Mr Heacock [Phillip Heacock (c1775-1851) Agent to the Devonshire Buxton Estate]. *We dined at five. Before dinner I went out in the chair and called at Mrs Bentley's. Mr Buxton at John's desire came to see me. He examined my legs and feet and ordered me to try the bath of the natural heat tomorrow. I sat alone some of the evening and John walked out with Mr Harrison, etc., etc.*

11th JULY

Got up very early. John left me for Hopton at 7. Breakfasted early - sent off two letters and before 11 o'clock went to the bath. It seemed to agree with me very well but I did not remain in it more than two minutes as I began to be shivery. After returning to the Inn I dressed, wrote a little and read. Mrs Harrison called and Henrietta went out riding with her. Mr Buxton called to see me after the bath which I must take again on Wednesday. Bessy [lady's maid] *made her appearance on Saturday and I wrote home to say I shou'd keep her as I was going into lodgings. I sent her out to buy some necessaries as I go to my new domicile to night Dined at the hotel and then took a ride round the plantation and got out at the lodgings which I think I shall like very well. The sitting room is a very good one and the bedroom tolerable. I paid my bill at St Anne's for the week £9.18s. 9d. I feel thank full I am rid of such heavy charges.*

12th JULY

Slept comfortably but feel as if I had taken a little cold. Saw Mrs Harrison who took Henny with her a walk and afterwards sent to ask her to go a drive. Who should be in the house but the late Miss Fanny Colquhoun now Mrs Ellis Ashton when I return'd from my ride she sent me her card and called upon me. I was never introduced before to her tho' I have frequently seen her and Mrs Henry and William know her. She is the lady whom both John and I admired when we have seen her walking round the Crescent.

13th JULY

A very cold day - very glad of a fire. A quiet comfortable day after a nice bath which seemed to agree very well with me. I walked with help to the end of the room and back. - Mr Buxton called told me to try the water with the addition of a little spirit of sweet nitre. In the evening I went out in the chair - the band played in the Crescent. Mr & Mrs Harrison talked with me a short time but it was too cold to stand long and I cou'd not have Joseph [the 'Boots' at the St Anne's Hotel] *to night - they had so much company.*

14th JULY

Read and worked all day after taking a bath early this morning. In the evening Mrs & Miss Harrison called and staid an hour they prevented me going out so soon as I intended, but I was out as late as I durst stay as it got very cold. I tried the water but I felt very shivery and uncomfortable most of the day afterwards, whether owing to it or not I know not.

15th JULY

I am prevented again bathing as I do not feel well independant of thermotism [a medical treatment involving the application of heat to the body] *-my stomach aches too violently to go into the water for some time. Much to my surprise, for the morning had been boisterious with violent storms of rain and thunder at a distance, just before dinner* (2 o'clock) *Michael came in, it was too late to add anything to a mutton chop. Fortunately we had plenty for in the middle of our meal my dear Husband also came in from Tissington - this was quite an unexpected pleasure. He also dined on chops and really had a better dinner if a fine meal had been prepared. The afternoon was so incessantly wet that it was impossible for any one to go out. After eight it cleared and Michael started home. A Gentleman wanted John, it was to make a will for a lady who is dying at Mr Clayton's lodgings - his evening was so spent mine in reading and working. Amelia Crossland called I have not seen her since Monday.*

6th JULY

John left me after Breakfast. Alone reading and writing. Amelia came in the evening but no Miss Woods. They were going to the Theatre with a brother and as Amelia seemed to wish to accompany them I asked her to take Henrietta with her. Therefore I had a lonely ride in the garden and on the Terrace in fact I was almost the only one out as the evening was very cold indeed I was driven in a short time by rain. Olive has had a letter from her Mother to tell her that her Brother is gone to Stafford for sheep stealing - he is sure to be transported for life. She does nothing but cry and can scarcely tell what she is doing. She will not be of much use to me I think but poor soul I pity her much.

17th JULY

Rose with a bad headache - took medicine feel very indifferent and Olive looks wretchedly. I have told her she may go to her Mother to accompany her to Stafford to see her Brother. I shou'd think it unfeeling if in her situation I was prevented going and I must try to do to others as I wou'd wish to be done to myself. I scarcely know what I am to do without her but must manage as well as I can. At present I do not know if she or Maria [another maid] *will return to me. Bessy will be but a poor Lady's Maid, someone else I must have.*

I have been watching all the gay people flocking to church how long it is since I was there and how much longer it may be it is impossible to guess. Buxton seems fuller of company than it was the beginning of the week. Amelia Crossland and her friend the Miss Woods drank tea with me Amelia staid supper. A wet day almost entirely and I never went out. This evening a Lady lodging next door who came for the recovery of her health departed this life. She is a Mrs Armistead of Grange near Holmes Chapel. About 8 Olive having met with a person from Leek walked home with him.

18th JULY

A very stormy day with violent showers. Maria arrived in the gig about half past one - left all well at home. Alone all day excepting Mrs Ashton who sat with me half an hour. Out for a short time in the bath chair but did not feel well. Wrote to my sister by today's post.

19th JULY

Mrs Harrison sat with me an hour today. Expected Amelia to spend the day but she did not come till after dinner and at last was driven away by Mr Buxton calling. I asked him to send me a little medicine for night. A very wet morning but rather cleared in the afternoon and I went out after tea till the rain drove me in. Wind has been for some time South West and the Barometer still drops, no prospects of fine weather yet.

20th JULY

I took blue pills last night, black draught this morning. My stomach better but still feel poorly and I think my feet are swelling again more than usual. The post boy who went to Leek brought me back some provisions, etc., etc, and a note from my dear Hub saying he thought he shou'd be with me tonight perhaps as late as 10 o'clock. I have sat with the blinds up waiting tea till after but he comes not so at eleven my carrier will take me to bed. Mrs Ashton paid me a long visit this afternoon she is a most agreeable pleasing Lady-like woman.

Went out to hear the band but found it colder than I have felt it for months, was glad of my fur cloak. Was introduced to Mr Ashton, a fit companion for his charming wife I know not when I have seen so pleasing a couple in appearance and manners. Mrs Harrison sent me a most beautiful bunch of flowers and she and Mr Harrison joined me on the terrace but it was too cold to stand talking. There were many gay people black satins, etc. and shoes and stockings fit to let in a famous fit of rheumatism - every one looked cold and pinched and the sensible people might be easily recognised by being well wrapped up. Mrs H. told me of a party who arrived at St Ann's this afternoon and who had left in the lobby of the hotel at Bakewell their money contained in a small tin box. A strange way of carrying money about and stranger forgetfulness to leave it behind, but they sent a person for it and recovered it, which was almost more than they deserved I think.

21st JULY

I went out in the bath chair for a short time it was so damp John wou'd not let me stay long. He is very much annoyed at being obliged to go to Stafford and the business is very unpleasant it arises out of a letter John received from the Rev. Mr Jones of Alton and he is called upon to produce it to prove a libel on a Mr Mason.

22nd JULY

Again a very wet disagreeable day. John left about seven, the corpse of the Lady who died at the next door was also taken at the same time. Almost as soon as I was carried downstairs and in a bathing dishabille was seated with my feet on the fender the door opened and Mrs and Miss Harrisons were announced. They came to take leave as they leave today. I was rather provoked being caught such a figure and again after bathing. I went out in the evening but the damp fell too thickly to be of service. Mrs Bentley came to tell me she had seen Mr Buxton and that he desired I wou'd go in which I soon did.

23rd JULY

As the morning was finer than usual and as John said he shou'd go to Stafford today I thought it probable Michael, etc. might come. I bathed again today but did not walk quite so well perhaps took a *little cold last night. I dined at three and ordered the carriage at ¹/₂ past four. Just as I was getting my bonnet on who shou'd make their appearance but my dear Husband and Mr Flint the latter thinks I am very much improved since he was here last. He has given me a prescription and has ordered me to be shampooed. They went out with me to hear the band but Mr F. complained sadly of the cold. I gave him something to revive him, however, for John dragged me up the hill in front of the Crescent and I called him to push at the back: I also had the honour of being carried upstairs by him. We had tea and they then left me to self and solitude. Mr Buxton called this morning.*

24th JULY

A very wet day - never went out. I made my first call on Mrs.Ashton today. Mrs Bentley called.

25th JULY

Again a wet showery day. Bathed. In the evening went out for an hour but found it very cold and damp. I heard from my dear sister yesterday her letter dated it from Brighton. Engaged Mrs Ainley to come and shampoo me tomorrow. I was jumped upon today for the first time and felt very poorly after.

26th JULY

A fine morning - wished to have had a ride early as I fixed not to bathe but the little carriage was engaged and only went out for an half an hour. Whilst on the terrace Michael, his wife, the childrens nurse and Olive arrived - all looking well. They intended going to Southport on Tuesday next. We dined and then took a walk (I rode) round the walks. Mr Cockburn came to tea. They left at ¹/₂ eight. Olive remained with me and Maria returned home. Mary brought me a letter from John which was written on Sunday. He begs I will leave off taking Gin and water at night. I therefore must do so as Mr Flint has given me a substitute in medicine. Mrs Ainley rubbed.

27th JULY

Bathed and at 12 Mrs Ainley came. Felt rather dull today being quite alone. Mrs Ashton sat with me a short time after dinner. I have felt sore after rubbing today.

28th JULY

Last night the first ball took place. The servants went with Mrs Ashton's to see the dancers consequently I was late in bed but I slept well and rose in famous spirits the morning was so fine and warm. I last night heard the band play and again this morning. After I came in Mrs Ainly operated not agreeably I must say for it gives me a good deal of pain. As soon as we had our dinner I went out in the bath chair and sat in the garden Olive occasionally drawing me. When Joseph came I went on the Terrace had a long chat with Mr & Mrs Ashton. They were at the ball and for the first of the season it was considered a pretty good one there being 28.

It was the first time they had seen the Galoppe danced and Mr A though it most revolting as the Ladies are thrown from the arms of one Gentleman into those of another like playing at Shuttlecock. It was danced by Sir James Ferguson's son, his cousin Miss Dundas and Mr Spencer the clergyman here and his wife - a fitting exhibition for Ministers of the Gospel. The Ashtons are not ball goers but he wished her to see the rooms. They are very amusing in their remarks, most agreeable and pleasant unaffected companions and I feel truly sorry they are talking of leaving on Saturday next.

Altogether I have enjoyed myself much this fine day but I shall not sit working in the garden again as I was almost devoured by gnats.

29th JULY

I felt so much stiffer and sorer today that when I returned from the bath Mrs Ainly was unwilling to rub me lest she shou'd bring on a fit of the Gout. Indeed the whole of the day I have felt very poorly indeed. The weather being very wet again I never stirred out. Olive wants to know if I will not go to a ball before I leave. Independent of not liking such amusements I am effectually debarred from joining them. I shall feel thankful if I can crawl out instead of crawling into the ballroom. Tho' I partake not of gaiety, I hear there was a grand display of conjuring at the Hall last night. Mrs Ashton called to say goodbye I parted with regret there is no one here now to whom I can exchange an idea.

30th JULY

We have had a very boisterous night and I spent it wakefully having touches of Gout in my heels and elbows. I believe there has been thunder but this I did not hear, the wind was too loud and the rain beat in torrents against the windows for one to distinguish distant sounds. I rose very undecided about bathing, but still at my usual hour I went. I was however like the cripple at the pool of Bethesda. Some Lady made her way first into the bathroom began to undress and it was impossible to oust her tho' I had been waiting 20 minutes and it wanted some time before the hour she had fixed for her bathing. This decided me however. I returned to my lodgings and declined making a second attempt and I was glad the Lady behaved so little like one as both Mr Buxton who called this morning and Mrs Ainly thought it better I shou'd not bathe today. I also again missed rubbing from the same cause-it was better not to be operated on.

Mr & Mrs Ashton left soon after ten and Sir Charles Scudamore is expected to take their rooms to night. I have been hearing some rather amusing anecdotes of this same fashionable Dr who seems to be walking the same path of impudence and adventure in which his predecessor Dr Driver so successfully played his part. It appears he will get into notice and into practice by some means or other and he not being very particular in his road to advancement becomes a character of celebrity in meeting rebuffs and not very gentle hints of dimissal. One rather amused me it being a good way of getting rid of a fee-loving Physician.

Two Gentlemen with whom he travelled from London in the coach (last year I believe) saying they were going to stop at Buxton for their health began a conversation with a Mr Simpson (Sir Charles' name when he wishes to be incognito to avoid the pay to ostlers, etc. expected from a Sir Charles). This continued at times during the journey. Of course he stopped also and pleasant companions being unwilling to part he offered to call upon them at their lodgings on the Hall Bank. Of course very happy, etc. he called, then announced his title, his profession, thought he cou'd be of benefit to them, gave each a prescription for which he received a sovereign each. Call after call, sovereign after sovereign until each gent had paid 11 sovereigns each. They then began to look seriously at each other -wondered where it wou'd end. At last they hit on this expedient to get him off his prey - they rose early -called the maid -told her Sir Charles wou'd call at such an hour as usual - to say they were out. He wou'd then enquire at which hour they wou'd return as he wished to see them, etc. So it exactly happened but instead of the maid saying when they wou'd return she told him she did not know but if he asked she was to tell him they were out but had each of them left his fee for him on the table which he might take that being the object of his call. This was too plain to be mistaken he turned on his heel and they never had the honour of a visit from him again.

I began to think Sir Charles wou'd not be my fellow lodger as he and Mrs Boam have been quarrelling this afternoon -he wanting to have a room for nothing. She told him he might go where he wou'd get cheaper lodging and put her ticket up again in the window but his luggage came in the evening and he soon after. Her Ladyship comes in about a week. She strives to get things for nothing it seems from all accounts. I have felt not quite so low in spirits today as I did yesterday.

I went out at 5 to hear the band and staid till after seven the evening proving fine. When I was seated under the piazza I observed a lady looking earnestly at me but as I was sure I had never seen her before I paid little attention to the circumstances. At last she came up to me asked if my name was Cruso came from Leek, etc. and of course I answered in the affirmative. She then introduced herself to me as Mrs Grey said she had often wished to see me and cou'd not then miss the opportunity of speaking to me (my astonishment increasing all the time) and thanking me very gratefully for the kindness I had formerly shown to her two nephews James and Tom Smith. Here the mystery was over. I remembered having heard them speak of Aunt Grey.

31st JULY

I got up aching and "Oh dearing". Soon after I was downstairs my dear Husband made his appearance. We have had a snug comfortable day together. In the evening went out for an hour and afterwards we read the bible to each other. I am only sorry I must so soon part with him again. He brought me some pills. Mr Gell sent me a certain cure for Gout and Rheumatism from which he has derived very great benefit during his late attack at Edinburgh. He speaks in high terms of them and of the maker who attended him. At any rate by the time he reached Hopton, to which place he was induced to come from his illness, he found himself quite well and ready to start back again to Scotland. I shall begin to take them tomorrow tonight I am going to take a powder of Mr Flints as I have had three very indifferent nights.

Again has my dear Husband supplied my want in the money way. I have made heavy demands upon him during my long stay here and I trust with God's blessing on the means I may be restored to health and be enabled by a constant kind love and affection to him return my gratitude to him for all his dear kindness to me. Few women have such kind husbands as mine. He does not strike me as looking or appearing well and his breath is much too feverish for health.

1st AUGUST

I felt so unwell today and had so much pain that I was afraid of going into the tepid bath and took my own and Mrs Ainleys advice and went to the Warm Bath instead which I think has been of benefit.

2nd AUGUST

A fine day after a rainy morning. I did not bath today but I have fixed for Mrs Ainley to come again tomorrow. I continue to have more pain but she tells me that is generally the case at first, therefore I shall continue the rubbing system.

3rd AUGUST

I was rubbed before I went to the bath. More helpless in my limbs - I fear I shall not be able to walk round the Crescent before I leave. Have been out twice in the carriage - went to hear the band at night.

4th AUGUST

Mrs Ainley the first thing - did not bathe- took a little medicine as I find these Edinburgh pills require it. Felt very poorly today. Went to hear the band at 11 in the afternoon went out again.

5th AUGUST

Durst not bathe today. Went out for an hour or two a fine day. At 5 exactly John and his father came to dinner and left me at 7 o'clock. I felt a little better today. I have had Mrs Ainley.

6th AUGUST

A most delightful day. Took a little more medicine and not feeling well with it went to the hot bath. Much stiffer and more pain. The last day -I am hesitating about going home the beginning of the week or remaining till the day originally fixed. I feel almost afraid of being laid up again and of being unable to be moved. I think I shall speak to Mr Buxton and go by his advice. Am obliged to sit up the greater part of the day as a recumbent posture is more painful and this was the case when I first began 11 weeks ago. Mrs Ainley this morning.

7th AUGUST

A beautiful glorious Sabbath. As I sit in my bedroom I can see numbers flocking to the House of God. I have spent most of the day in reading Mead's little work and like it much. I took blue pills last night I am better for it but very full of pain and can scarcely move one foot before the other again I have been out in the Bath chair twice for a short time. I was obliged to send Mrs Ainley back I felt too poorly for her.

8th AUGUST

Mrs Ainley came this morning. I found I was a little easier after she rubbed me but it was only for a short time and I became full of pain and helpless as ever. I was obliged to be lifted in and out of the bathchair. I was in the Garden for an hour and a half in the afternoon and in the evening went out for a short time only. Mrs Bentley called whilst I was at dinner and sat with me until I went out I was very ill when I went to bed.

9th AUGUST

I passed a better night than I expected but was unable to move and lay in one position all night. When I awoke I found I had Gout in my left heel. Mrs Ainley came but durst not touch me. The morning was so beautiful I was lifted into the chair and sat on the Terrace until the band had finished playing.

11th AUGUST

At nine o'clock Michael came to breakfast on his way to the moors to join John. I have been very ill with pain all day I sent for Mr Buxton last night but he did not come. I went out to hear the band and as soon as it had finished playing I came in again as I can scarcely bear the shaking and am soon tired of the position. In fact I am quite as ill as I was at the commencement of this attack and I am sure Buxton has been of no service and something else must be tried if I am to get well. Olive went to the play she was treated by Mr Moore but seemed not much amused. I sent again for Mr Buxton to come in the morning.

12th AUGUST

A lovely day for the sportsmen I met on Wednesday evening Mr Besant and Messrs Roland and John Heathcote. They were on their way to the same moors that John goes to. Mr Buxton called but as I was just dressing he went away after speaking to Sir Charles Scudamore about a patient he wished him to see and said he wou'd call about 10 o'clock. I staid in till 4 and he did not come. Whilst I was sitting in the Garden he came to me and told me he wou'd come in the morning. As it happened I was sorry for by to-days post I received a letter from Margaret Cruso saying John was bringing Mr Walker [another doctor] to see me on Saturday Evening and if I staid longer at Buxton she wou'd come and nurse me. It is very kind of her indeed but I hope I may go home. I have been nearly 7 weeks here I shall be delighted to find myself there again. I certainly shall regret the perfect quiet of this place [it] suits me as does also the solitude in which I live. I find myself so perfectly helpless and withal that, have generally so much pain that company however intimate I find, if too long bestowed on me, a great means of tiring and wearying me. I verily believe, to hear others laugh and talk and move about tho I may be sitting quietly silent, gives me a degree of irritation from which I suffer a good deal afterwards, for I must try to exert myself and do so with no good effect.

13th AUGUST

Mr Buxton called, talked looked at my feet and did nothing. He was told that Mr Cruso was bringing a Medical man to see me and he said he wou'd call again before I left. About 7 John and Michael made their appearance in half an hour afterwards Mr Walker and he came in true Buxton style, limping. He had had a jerk out of his gig and tho' not much hurt the wheel catch'd his side and he was stiff and lame. I had been tired with my visitors and worse I proved tonight than ever he therefore saw me in perfection. He examined my feet and legs and said he did not wonder my spirits were not lowered with such wear and tear for it is 12 weeks today since I have been able to walk and almost I may say move.

14th AUGUST

Mr W[alker] examined my back thigh, etc. and said I shou'd never be well until a counter irritation was produced. He has ordered me to go home -Buxton never likely to be of use as long as the complaint was unmoved- to be cupped, then blistered to be kept open for a week, then cupped and if the pain not gone which he thinks it will not I must have an issue put into my hip. In fact I must suffer much more to be cured than I have hitherto done and he has no hesitation in saying these things should have been done before I ever came here. If I do not use these means and let it go on he says I should be a cripple for life and he thinks I shall always be liable to attacks which always must be seriously and severely dealt with. He left after breakfast. John and Michael went to church where the Annual Charity Sermon was presented by the Dean of Litchfield Mr Howard brother to Lord Carlisle. We dined at 3 - went out for a short time and my gents left at 6. After church I went on the terrace for a short time. The evening has been delightful and I cou'd have staid out much longer with pleasure if I had durst to do so.

15th AUGUST

Rather a dull morning, but no rain. I hoped to have bathed but was prevented. In the afternoon, for I dined early, I went and sat in the gardens with my book. Much to my surprise when there I was startled from a reverie in Edward Thompson's battle burst by John's and Michael's voices. They came many hours earlier than I expected having risen at $^1/_2$ past two in the morning for the purpose of bagging a good number of grouse and never having a shot they left the moors, dined at Castleton on their road and came to drink tea with me. They drew the bath chair for me and I remained out till dusk. I was in much pain all day and cou'd scarcely bear the motion of the little carriage -what shall I do tomorrow on my return over the hills?

16th AUGUST

The carriage came early. John went out to call on and pay Mr Buxton -more money required to leave

Buxton out of debt. We went into the Crescent to hear the band - whilst there introduced to Mr Heacock [Duke of Devonshire's Agent at Buxton]. *He stood talking with us much of the time. In a gig tandem driven into the Crescent appeared Sir Francis Burdett and another Gentleman. They had great difficulty in getting taken in into any place Buxton is so full. At last Mr Heacock got them admitted at the Great Hotel but there was no room excepting the Card room into which they were ushered. John decided to speak to Sir Charles Scudamore about me before we left accordingly I had to see him, tell all particulars, etc. He wished I had done so before as he was sure he cou'd be of service to me but he told me time wou'd be necessary to eradicate the painful complaint. He sent a prescription and wrote a long letter to Mr Flint. He does not recommend cupping but blisters and aqua punctuation to my feet. As soon as he had delivered the letter to me we started -John and I inside Jacques and Olive out. Michael took Bessy in the gig, the dog waggon all my household comforts in the shape of leg rest, pillows, etc. I arrived at home about five but felt wearily tired tho' I did not find the carriage shake me as much as I expected. A crowd of course collected to see me carried into the house and I will engage many reports are even now afloat about me...'* [27]

Despite bathing and a course of massage it would seem that Mary Cruso's gout was not improved by her seven week stay at Buxton. It is interesting to observe that, whilst she took advice from her several medical practitioners, she remained in control of her own treatment and mixed hot and cold bathing with patent medicines such as 'Edinburgh' and blue pills, and other medications of the time, such as colchicum and sweet nitre (saltpetre). The diary demonstrates very vividly early 19th century medical practice where baths and bathing, including massage, might give temporary relief but no effective treatment was available, and where medical opinions differed significantly and doctors were predisposed to trial and error.

The Hot Baths in the early 1840s

The Hot Baths produced a clear profit of about £300 a year from the time they were built into the 1840s and expenditure on maintenance averaged £60 p a. The baths were fed from the natural mineral springs into a cistern enclosed within a larger cistern and, between the two, steam was circulated to heat the water to a temperature of about 95°F. (35°C) The most expensive operating outlay was for coal and expenditure on the boiler also tended to be high so, clearly, the provision of hot baths was quite a costly operation. But the baths were popular and by 1840 the facilities had been doubled to 2 baths for gentlemen and 2 for ladies with a vapour and shower bath for each.

The expansion may have taken place in 1836/7 when there was increased expenditure including the provision of a new office. T.J. Page, writing in 1843, made special mention of the vapour and shower baths at Buxton. He suggested that the vapour (or steam) bath was an effective treatment for gout, rheumatism, fever, liver complaints and incipient consumption amongst other complaints and that the bathing regime might be from 20 to 30 minutes in a bath of between 120°F to 130°F. (48.5-55° C.) He observed that shower baths were, perhaps, the most unexceptionable mode of bathing but, nevertheless, went on to say '...*When there is a natural determination of blood to the head, I know no means so generally effectual in restoring the balance of circulation as a course of shower bathing...*'.

T.J.Page also mentioned the operation of 'shampooing' as part of the water treatment and recommended Mr Joseph Miller of the Market Place, Buxton as a skilful practitioner in the art of 'shampooing and galvanizing'. Miller described himself as an 'anatomical shampooer' and this is, of course, massage (though the word had yet to come into common parlance). By 1842 there were a number of such shampooers some resident and some who visited the town in the season. As demand grew these medical assistants became resident in Buxton and worked in association with the doctors, giving hot-air, shower and vapour baths as well as various forms of shampoo or massage.

The Beauties of Buxton

In 1841 John Bates Chambers, who ran a toy and fancy goods shop in Spring Gardens, produced a second edition of his *Beauties of Buxton, or New and Improved Visitors' Guide to that Celebrated watering Place* in which he paints a colourful picture of life for the visitor to the town:

'*...The rising ground, in front of the Crescent, is laid out in a succession of terraces... these intersect the hill in every direction, communicating with each other by numerous flights of steps, and are ornamented with a number of beautiful urns. These walks form the favourite promenade of the visitors, and on a summers day, when the band is playing, are generally crowded with company, affording an interesting sight for a reflective mind. The lower walks are generally occupied by invalids, these, though coming from different quarters, and total strangers to each other, by a sort of free-masonry, very soon get aquainted; for there is something in affliction which speedily brings fellow-sufferers together, and here they may often be seen in groups of half-a-dozen or upwards, very generally comparing notes, and reporting progress, - and it is not a little amusing (for they are frequently very facetious for persons in their condition,) to sit and listen to their conversation. One will be showing the rest how much higher he can lift his arm than he could the preceding day; another boasting that he has left one of his crutches at his lodgings, having supplied its place by a stick, and that he purposes leaving the other there on the morrow. Occasionally a challenge to a race of twenty or thirty yards on the gravelled walk will be given and accepted by two of the party. The preliminaries being settled, off they start at a tortoise speed-stopped every step or two, by a sudden twinge, which calling forth an exclamation of pain, commonly elicits some waggish remark from the rest. One of them, most generally, breaking down by the way, the other is declared victor,-the loser covering the mortification of defeat by assuring his competitor that he shall be ready for a fresh trial of strength on the morrow, and expressing his confidence that, in the next attempt, the wreath awarded to successful racers will deck his brow. Thus do they endeavour, and successfully too, to cheat affliction of that sadness which she so frequently imposes upon her victims, and beguile away many an otherwise monotonous hour.*

But let us take the higher terrace. There, apart from the more joyous circles, and, apparently, choosing to be alone, is a young man reclining on one of the seats. It is summer weather and the sun is shining; yet is he wrapped in a coat or cloak. By his side is a female. As we approach he turns his head; and his pallid cheek and sunken eye tell a sad tale of woe. We see consumption has commenced her fearful ravages; and, in imagination, we revert to the home he has left but a few days before. We see the anxiety of the parents as the insidious disease gains ground; various remedies are tried in vain. As a last resource, the physician advises a visit to Buxton, hoping that a change of air, together with fresh scenery and society, may accomplish what medicine has failed to effect. And now hath he come hither, attended by his mother or sister in the capacity of nurse. Poor sufferer! may the invigorating breeze which fans thy pale brow bring strength to thy enfeebled frame; and, restored to heath, mayest though return home, adding another unit to the thousands who have received benefit from a visit to Buxton. As we gain the higher ground , our steps are impeded, and our reflections interrupted, by the crowded state of the walks. Gay and smiling groups succeed each other. Here a circle of young girls, who have never been from home before, are enraptured

The Serpentine Walks

with all they see and hear; there, two parties on meeting recognise each other as old friends or school-
fellows. Mutual exclamations of surprize soon give way to hasty interrogatories: "When did you arrive?"-
"Where are you lodging?" &c. &c., and much pleasure is anticipated from the unexpected meeting. A seat,
here, is filled with gentlemen who are busily discussing politics, or some other topic of the day; there, a bevy
of ladies ...are engaged in earnest conversation.. Other parties of maturer ladies are engaged in fasionable
chit-chat, or in admiring the splendid equipages as they roll out of the Crescent area...'[28]

Dr Augustus Bozzi Granville toured the spas of England in 1839-40. He found Buxton to
positively exude the air of aristocracy and was admonished by the proprietress of the Great Hotel for
having written a book on the Spas of Germany which had lured important visitors to German spas thus
causing her to lose business. He was generally very favourable in his description but he was not
impressed with the service of drinking water at St Anne's Well;

'...Early the following morning I proceeded to taste the water at the well, which is sheltered by a
low Grecian canopy, where I saw many who attended to do the same; but they were all ordinary people,
who deposited their penny contribution upon the stone-flag that covers the source. I saw non of the
"creme de la societe" drinking the tepid spring; - but perhaps it was too early, as few people were
abroad... A nearly decrepit old woman seated before the scanty stream, with her shrivelled hands
distributes it to the applicants as they approach her...'

He compares the old Buxton Well Women with the smartly dressed female attendants in Germany
and suggests that Buxton should provide much more elegant facilities for the drinking of the water. This
would encourage more of the superior class of visitor who tend to have the water sent to their apartment
rather than present themselves at the well. He also bemoans the lack of a promenade-room for those
drinking the water and suggests that the promenade and reading room in the Crescent at that time was
a much inferior facility for a spa of Buxton's reputation.[29]

In another ten years Dr Granville would have seen a transformation in the baths provision in the town.

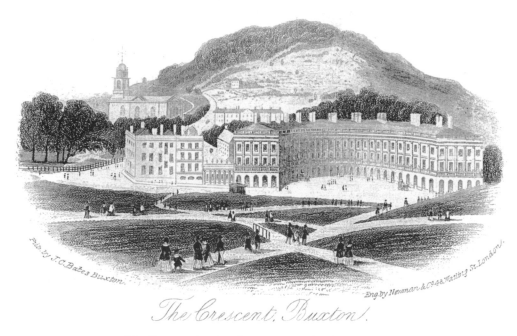

The Crescent, Buxton!

The Crescent showing the new Natural baths of 1851-54

The Major Rebuild of the Baths 1851-1854

The Great Exhibition of 1851 in Hyde Park clearly showed the progress which Britain had made in innovation and industry in the 19th century, and it was to preface widespread wealth through new and expanded industries. Buxton had enjoyed steady, if not spectacular, growth through the first half of the century, exemplified by the extension of the bathing arrangements, but the second half of the century was to see the town really expand as an inland spa. Between 1849 and 1852 the Royal Hotel was built, the largest and most important building since the Square. The Royal, designed by the Sheffield architect Samuel Worth, and built for the solicitor Andrew Brittlebank, was an early piece of private development in the town. It was to be followed by the Quadrant built as individual private investments between 1853 and 1864 but retaining the same architectural style to the front curved facade.

The decision to invest in a complete rebuild of the Hot and Natural Baths was probably taken in 1851 and Joseph Paxton, designer of the Great Exhibition's Crystal Palace and close confidante of the 6th Duke of Devonshire, had more than a passing interest in this development at Buxton. The remodelling of the Baths was carried out to the designs of Henry Currey, the Duke of Devonshire's architect. The Natural Baths old buildings were pulled down in early 1852 and by April work was progressing rapidly. The designs for the external facade of the two buildings were very different but the construction of the roofs at both the Hot and Natural Baths involved the same glass 'ridge and furrow' principle.

The principle contractors were London firms with Sanders & Woolcott responsible for the main contract, William Jeakes of Bloomsbury for the major plumbing and Mr Riddell carrying out the plastering of the Hot Wing. The ironwork to the Hot Wing was, however, provided by John Walker of York. *The Builder* magazine of August 20th 1853 carried the following description:
'...The Baths consist of two distinct buildings...both being approached under cover (a point of much importance for invalids)... one is called the "natural wing" from the water being used there

The Natural Baths newly rebuilt in 1854

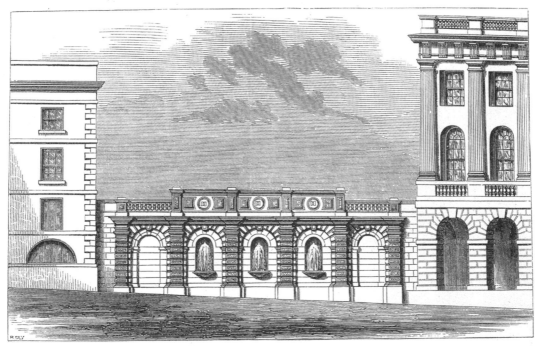

South Front of the New Ranges of Natural Baths at Buxton, showing the connection of the Baths with the West End of the Crescent.

The Hot Baths newly rebuilt in 1854

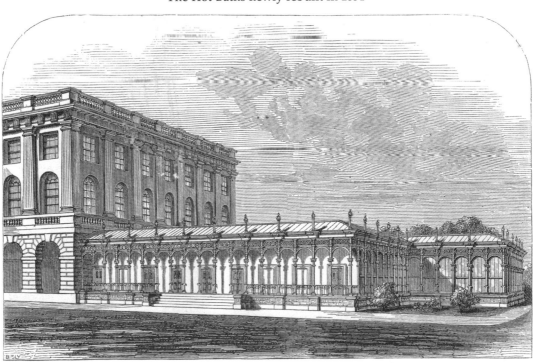

South and West Fronts of the New Ranges of Hot Baths at Buxton, showing the connection of the Baths with the East End of the Crescent.

at its natural temperature; the other the "hot wing" where the temperature is artificially raised to any required extent. The tepid springs issue from the limestone rocks immediately under the site of the natural wing, and some of the baths are supplied through perforations in the marble bottoms which are laid hollow over the rock. The baths are built at such a level that the height to which the springs rise forms the required depth. A reservoir is formed at the principal source and the water flows continuously from there to the whole range of baths. The water is also led from the same service to a large reservoir under the hot wing to supply that building but here the water has to be pumped up into tanks to supply the different baths. It was deemed of great importance to have the natural wing built immediately over the springs, so that the gases in the water might escape as little as possible. The ground is of an irregular shape, and part of the baths are formed in the lower storey of the Old Hall Hotel...

...Wide corridors... are sufficiently commodious to serve as waiting rooms. Two dressing rooms are provided to each private bath which gives an opportunity of working them more expeditiously. Douche, shower, vapour and commodious charity baths for both sexes are provided in each wing with distinct entrances. A room for drinking the tepid waters from St Anne's Well and another for drinking a strong chalybeate, brought from a hill adjoining, are provided in the same building.

The natural wing, from the character of the site, exhibits only one facade, executed in the stone of the neighbourhood of a rich warm colour, and there being no windows or doors in it, three fountains in fluted niches are introduced to give life to the elevation. The hot wing, which exhibits two considerable facades, is constructed in iron and glass, producing a variety, and enabling the architect to give the utmost degree of lightness and cheerfulness to the interior. The roofs are formed on the 'ridge and furrow' principle in 9 and 10 feet spans... the whole is glazed with Hartley's 'rough plate'... sun blinds are provided internally... the baths are lined with patent glazed porcelain bricks... the bottoms are formed with veined Sicilian marble and the whole of the private and douche baths in the hot wing are formed with similar marble... the natural wing is warmed by means of hot water, and the hot wing by steam from the boilers...' [30]

This is a detailed account from which we learn some important points. The Baths were clearly completed quite quickly, substantially between April 1852 and August 1853. The Devonshire Buxton accounts indicate that the baths remained open for business during the rebuild and there is a note in the 1853 accounts which refers to the extra expense incurred in keeping both the old and the new Hot Baths open during the season. The article describes how the water was routed to the Hot Baths and that a pump was required to raise it to the level required. This, as we shall see, was an expensive process, expenditure on coal being one of the greatest operating costs.

The *Builder* article also states quite clearly that the roofing of both Baths was on the glazed 'ridge and furrow' principle. The use of ridge and furrow roofing was comparatively new in 1851, it had been invented by Joseph Paxton in the early 1830s as part of his design for conservatories. It has been argued that Paxton may have had some influence in the design of the Hot Baths in that the ridge and furrow roof and glazed sides were descendants of the Lily House which he designed at Chatsworth in 1849/50. Currey and Paxton had worked together on the Princes Park, Liverpool, in 1843 and Paxton had advised Currey on his design for the Long Conservatory at Chiswick in 1850, at the request of the Duke. Paxton was in Buxton supervising the Park layout at the same time as the baths were being built. Indeed, his plan for the Park included the new baths shaded in pink as were all the other proposed developments. The two architects were in Buxton together in September of 1852 when they toured all the new sites with the Duke of Devonshire. In a pamphlet reviewed in *The Lancet* in 1852, Dr W.H. Robertson observed that Sir Joseph Paxton had superintended the major rebuilding of the baths. It may be noted also that Currey did not use an iron and glass design in any of the several commissions he subsequently completed in Buxton and he was not responsible for the glass and iron pavilion of 1871, commissioned by the Buxton Improvements Company and designed by Edward Milner. So there is firm evidence for the influence of a newly-knighted Sir Joseph Paxton in the rebuild.[31]

The Natural Baths now offered two public and two private baths for men, effectively the original or Great Bath, which had always been a public bath, and the 1806 White Bath (which had previously been described as a private bath) formed the public bath provision. The ladies accommodation was one public and two private baths. Two well rooms for drinking purposes were provided, one for the natural mineral water and the other for chalybeate water. The baths were entered from corridors off the Crescent colonnade in between the two well rooms. There were also two Charity Baths, one each for male and female and these were entered from a yard at the back of the building. The Hot Baths offered one public and four private baths for men and the same for women and a public cold plunge bath. There were also two baths each for male and female charity patients which were entered from the rear of the building. Both sets of baths contained douche closets, dressing rooms and other facilities required for medical bathing.

Amongst the many items of furniture and equipment for the Baths were cocoa matting made at the New Bailey prison, Salford, a washing machine costing £7.7s.0d and a patent mangle which cost £15.15s.0d. In 1852 Dr Lyon Playfair was asked to carry out an analysis of the water and this was published and distributed by post to more than 3,500 addresses as part of the publicity for the baths. The new baths were a great success and were featured in an article with an engraving in the *Illustrated London News* of August 1854. In the same year Dr Robertson, Buxton's foremost authority on water treatment, published the first edition of his *Buxton Guide* in which he gave a full description of the baths and medical treatments. From the opening of the new baths to 1860 the Devonshire Buxton Estate took a clear profit on their operation of about £1800 per annum, the best year being 1856 when a clear profit of £2,187 was earned. During this time the bathman was paid £78 and the bathwoman £40 a year.[32]

The remodelling of the water facilities included the dismantling of the old St Anne's Well designed by Carr, though the urn which surmounted it was saved and can now be seen on the Devonshire Royal Hospital south front. The drinking well had become part of the Natural Baths complex and the well women continued to dispense the water, for which they received a gratuity. The requirements of the Enclosure Act meant that a separate free supply of the waters had to continue to be made available to the public. This was complied with in 1855 when the Buxton Estate paid £132 for the erection of a double pump which dispensed natural tepid water from one side and cold from the other.

Tonic or Cold Plunge Bath

Apart from the baths in the Crescent, Buxton had an additional bath served by natural spring sources. This was located at the bottom of Bath Road (at the corner of today's Macclesfield and Burlington Roads) and was known as the Tonic or Cold Plunge Bath. Despite the attempts of owners it had a rather chequered commercial career, being entirely overshadowed by the Natural Baths. The 1772 Enclosure Act records that it was situated on land owned by Dr Norton of Macclesfield. Pilkington, writing in

The Tonic Bath in about 1920 can be seen in the foreground with semi-circular roof

1789, describes: '...*other springs have been discovered, and that during last summer a scheme was in agitation for erecting buildings near them for the accommodation of company...*'[33]

A bath, measuring thirty feet by twelve feet, was built over these springs, which by 1797 had been divided to accommodate males and females separately. The temperature of this bath was nominally 63.8°F (17.7°C.) but it seemed that some difficulty was experienced in keeping the temperature stable since cold and tepid springs arose from various parts of the bath floor. Dr Denman suggested that attempts made to heat part of the bath by means of flues were only partly successful because no provision was made for diverting the cold water. Thus whilst the patient's trunk was immersed in heated water the colder spring was still emerging from the bath.[34]

Early in the 19th century Arthur Jewitt's *History of Buxton* described the bath in somewhat disparaging terms. He said that there were both warm and cold springs here but that, due to mismanagement these could never be properly separated and that the temperature was therefore 64°F (17.6°C) He suggests that the efforts made by Dr Norton to raise the temperature by means of flues was not only unsuccessful but was an attempt to deceive the public by substituting an artificial for a natural bath. This is being a little hard on Dr Norton since his heating arrangements were similar to those employed in the Gentlemen's Private Bath, as we have seen in chapter two. Indeed, after examining the Tonic Bath arrangements, Dr Denman had advocated the provision of hot baths twenty years before the Hot Baths were built in the Crescent. The Tonic Bath was essentially a cold bath, though there is a lack of consistency in the measurement of its temperature by writers in the early 19th century, with recordings varying between 60° F and 68° F (15.4° and 20°C.) Being natural cold springs, it is likely that the temperature would vary with the seasons. It was compared with the tepid springs at Matlock which were said to measure 68°F (20°C.) on average. The bath was fitted with a pump for the direct application of a spray of water to the bather.

The Tonic Bath interior in about 1947

The bath was described in 1819 as having water at a temperature of 60° (15.4°C.) and though it had previously been divided into separate sections for ladies and gentlemen, by that time was one single bath but with a floor of two different depths. In 1823 the bath was open but not much used and by 1835 it was being run by Mr William Moore. A guide book of 1842 suggested that whilst the accommodation offered at this bath was perfect and the terms moderate, nevertheless it was not much frequented since most people came to Buxton for the natural mineral waters and their medicinal properties.[35]

By 1847 the Tonic Bath was closed but it was again open in 1852 with William Boam as the bath keeper.[36] In November 1860 the bath and bathhouse were offered for sale by auction and from 1861 there is reference to this bath in the Devonshire Buxton accounts when a new drain was laid at a cost of just over £79 and William Boam paid £16 in rent.[37] It is likely that the Devonshire Buxton Estate had acquired the bath, for between 1862 and 1864 the estate paid for substantial repairs. The nature of the work suggests that the bath was re-excavated or enlarged, properly drained and covered with stonework and an iron roof. A new road to the bath, Bath Street, was laid and the total cost was just under £500 which included the architect, Henry Currey's fee. In 1865 an income statement for the Tonic Bath appeared in the Estate accounts for the first time at £4.16.0 and £16 was spent on repairs.

In 1866 the income was £11.16.0 and £24 was spent on repairs, mainly plumbing. In 1867 the income was not separately identified but the bath was only open for a short time for which James Boam, who was the attendant at the Natural Baths, was paid a small amount for attendance and washing at the Tonic Bath. A letter of complaint to *The Buxton Advertiser* in August 1867 confirms that the Tonic Bath was closed. It would seem that the Devonshire Buxton Estate had directly managed the bath for a short time but found it ran at a loss. However between 1868 and 1870 the Estate paid for further substantial work to be carried out, and on the house adjoining (probably Bath House), at a cost of just under £485, which included '...*new metal piping and setting the bath in order...*'

In 1869 William Boam, who had paid £16 per year rent for the Tonic Bath continuously from 1861, died, and from Michaelmas [September 29th] of that year Thomas Woodruff took on the lease, though at the considerably increased rent of £90.10s. Woodruff probably ran the bath as a private concern until 1881, though it was described as 'disused' on the 1878 survey plan. In 1882 the lease was taken by Thomas and M.B. Wilson at a rent of £50 pa., but although the accounts show that the Tonic Bath and house were given up from Ladyday [March 25th] 1881, Woodruff continued to pay a rent of £40 p.a. certainly until 1891.

In 1889 the Tonic Bath was referred to by name in a local guide, though other guides of 1891 to 1912 refer to it as a tepid swimming bath, a Buxton guide of 1896 describes: '...*the swimming bath at the end of Broad Walk is large and well kept and is supplied with limestone water at 60° F...*'[38]

In 1918-19 it was described as a swimming bath and by 1927-28 it was in use by the boys of Buxton College, at which time it was covered by a semi-cylindrical structure. This use, according to local residents, continued up to at least 1939, and it may also have been used by private schools in the town. From July 1946 the bath was acquired by the Spa Hotel who carried out some renovations and opened it on a club membership basis. Buxtonians who swam there remember the coldness of the water and the large cast iron pipes round the edge of the bath which were formerly used for heating. By 1969 the Spa Hotel had closed and with it the bath which has now been built over.[39]

Bathing Medicine

The range of treatments included bathing programmes (often associated with dietary regimes), douches or sprays on affected parts of the body (including the use of double-action force pumps) and also massage. John Pearson, a consulting surgeon at the Devonshire Hospital, set out reports of cases of treatment to charity patients in a booklet in 1861, of which the following are typical:

'....*CASE LXXXII*
M.B. Age 39, a Charwoman. August 18th 1860. Had Rheumatic Fever in January. Has now pain in all her joints - bowels costive - tongue white - pulse quick and feeble - slight cough - has palpitation sometimes when lying down. Ordered dose of physic - 3 warm baths.
August 25th. Less pain - feels better - continue warm baths.
September 1st. Bowels costive - physic - continue warm baths.
September 8th. Discharged. Much relieved

CASE LXXXV
P.C. age 53, a Weighing Clerk. August 18th 1860. This man was here in June and July; commenced being worse after getting home, and could not work. Ordered warm baths.
September 1st. Much better. Ordered natural baths and douche.
Remained until 26th, and went home Cured.[40]....'

During the major rebuild of the Natural Baths the medical practitioners had insisted that the design should allow for the natural mineral water to be used right over the spring sources. Dr Robertson was a keen advocate of this arguing that the effect of the water bubbling up through the floor of the bath was of itself extremely beneficial, and that baths sited away from the spring source (thus of a lesser temperature than the normal 82°F were much less effective in their treatment. Not all doctors held this view; Dr Carstairs observed that the Charity Baths were some distance from the spring source and thus of a slightly lower temperature yet great claims were made for the cure rate of charity patients. Dr Robertson maintained his stance and as we shall see later, this had a particular effect on the siting of the new Charity Baths in 1876. He advanced a very clever argument in respect of the Hot Baths saying that if you took water at a natural temperature of, say, 50°F, and heated it to 95°F, you would materially affect the characteristics of that water, whereas taking Buxton mineral water at 82°F required only a small amount of additional heat and this would be less likely to affect the medicinal properties of the water.

Dr Robertson wrote extensively on the effects of the Buxton natural mineral water. He asserted that the Buxton baths were most effective in cases of rheumatism, gout, neuralgia and certain forms of spinal, uterine and dyspeptic affections. He advised that no invalid should come to take the baths without the express advice and sanction of their usual medical attendant and furthermore that '...*medical men cannot be made too fully cognizant of the stimulating and alternative character of these mineral waters...*'

Robertson was careful also to protect his specialised knowledge indicating that only a medical person who had been closely associated with the use of such waters in medical treatment over a period of time could properly advise on treatments, therefore the patient should always use the waters under the direction of a medical man resident in Buxton. He was unequivocal in this advice saying '...*it is my duty to state this... and to urge it upon public attention; and the seniority of my position enables me to do this with a less chance of misconstruction, and justifies me in doing so...*'[41] Dr W.H. Robertson built a formidable medical reputation in Buxton over 60 years from 1837.

The Turkish Bath

By 1864 some changes had been made to the Hot Baths, though the Natural Baths remained much the same as in 1854. In the Hot Baths the Gentlemen's Large Hot Public Bath had been converted to private baths and the Cold Swimming Bath, projecting to the east side, had been closed, the accommodation used as a billiard room. These changes took place in 1860 at a cost of £161. The old billiard room was converted into a reading room which formed part of the business of J.C. Bates, the proprietor of *The Buxton Advertiser*, whose offices were in the Hot Baths Colonnade by 1864.

The most important change, however, was the introduction of a Turkish or Hot Air Bath department into the Hot Baths. The building work was carried out in 1861 and the baths were situated on the eastern side behind the former cold swimming bath. The building cost was £1082 and the architect, Henry Currey, was paid a fee of £61.12.0 for the design. By August of 1861 the Devonshire Buxton Estate were taking an income from the Turkish Baths though it was very modest and the venture was short-lived. In 1863 the manager Mr James Seeley left, and by June 1865 the baths were closed. The Turkish Baths simply did not pay; in fact the income derived was not even enough to cover the operating costs. It would seem that this form of bath was not popular in Buxton in the 1860s.

Hot Bath and Devonshire Colonnades

Within just a few years of opening it was recognised that the Hot Baths were a prime site for shops. In 1863 storerooms at the front of the building were converted into two shops, one of which was occupied by John Milligan the draper and the other by Thomas Woodfuff who ran a spar museum. We have already mentioned J.C. Bates and *The Buxton Advertiser* office and by 1864 there were five other shops in the newly formed Hot Bath Colonnade including J.W. Potter, hosier and W. Oram, fruiterer and poulterer. By 1866 the whole east side of the Hot Baths had been turned into shops to form a further new shopping amenity called the Devonshire Colonnade . The Baths building now housed five shops in the Hot Bath Colonnade and six in the Devonshire Colonnade.

The Hot baths and Devonshire Colonnade in the 1880s.

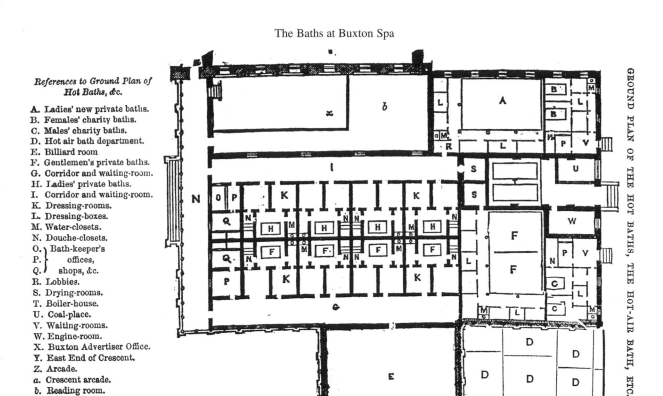

References to Ground Plan of Hot Baths, &c.

A. Ladies' new private baths.
B. Females' charity baths.
C. Males' charity baths.
D. Hot air bath department.
E. Billiard room
F. Gentlemen's private baths.
G. Corridor and waiting-room.
H. Ladies' private baths.
I. Corridor and waiting-room.
K. Dressing-rooms.
L. Dressing-boxes.
M. Water-closets.
N. Douche-closets.
O. ⎫ Bath-keeper's
P. ⎬ offices,
Q. ⎭ shops, &c.
R. Lobbies.
S. Drying-rooms.
T. Boiler-house.
U. Coal-place.
V. Waiting-rooms.
W. Engine-room.
X. Buxton Advertiser Office.
Y. East End of Crescent.
Z. Arcade.
a. Crescent arcade.
b. Reading room.

GROUND PLAN OF THE HOT BATHS, THE HOT-AIR BATH, ETC.

Plan of the Hot baths 1864 showing the Turkish or Hot Air Baths (marked 'D')

New Roofs to the Baths

Throughout the changes to the Hot Baths no significant changes were made to the Natural Baths until the re-roofing of 1865/6. The glass ridge and furrow roofing had proved to be uncomfortably hot in summer and excessively cold in winter as well as being prone to leaking. The glass was replaced with slates and skylights by a Manchester contractor, Robert Carlyle on a contract worth £1373 over two years. The architect for the work was Henry Currey though local supervision was provided by the surveyor to the Buxton Estate, Robert Rippon Duke. The contract did not run particularly smoothly and R.R. Duke entered into much correspondence with Robert Carlyle and with the Duke of Devonshire's Buxton Agent, George Drewry. At one point R.R. Duke tried to introduce local plumbers onto the job because the contractors were not getting on with the work to his satisfaction. It may be for this reason that similar re-roofing of the Hot Baths, which took place in 1868/9, was carried out by local tradesmen including the plumbing firm of Joseph Broomhead of Terrace Road. The re-roofing work on the Hot Baths cost more than at the Natural Baths though it also included widening the colonnade and other maintenance.

By 1870 the Baths were producing a combined income in excess of £5500 p.a. and showing a net profit of between £3500 and £4500 p.a., depending upon cost of maintenance and improvements. Typically about 59,000 baths would be taken in the year. In 1869/70 considerable work was undertaken at the Baths to increase the supply of water to both buildings. Additional reserve tanks were fitted at the Hot Baths and new connections made to the Natural building. The main contractor for the work was Edward Frith who had done other water engineering work for Buxton. The work, which also included a new boiler and heating tank at the Hot Baths, cost more than £1000 and was supervised by the estate surveyor, Robert R. Duke.

New Charity Baths

From 1870, profit on the baths continued to grow steadily and by 1875 a net profit of more than £5000 was achieved. Buxton was now a thriving spa with the baths supporting a wide range of services from bathchairmen to laundries and a comprehensive range of hotels and lodging houses to suit all tastes and pockets. The Devonshire Buxton Estate was deriving a good income from the baths and the agent, George Drewry, was obviously keen to enhance their commercial viability, hence the investments made on the Hot Baths and the attempts in the early 1870s to increase the flow of water.

For some time the agent had been attempting to find alternative bathing accommodation for the Charity patients so that their not inconsiderable facilities could be converted to provide additional accommodation for paying patients. He was concerned that the Baths were becoming overcrowded and in an editorial article in *The Advertiser* of November 28th 1874, it was observed that the Hot and Natural Baths had been so incredibly overcrowded in the past year that it was vital that extra space be found for more baths.

Various suggestions were put forward including the use of vacant land at the back of the Crescent as a site for additional baths and it was noted that some years previously consideration had been given to moving the Charity Baths to the Devonshire Hospital - plans had been drawn up for George Drewry by both the hospital architect, Robert R. Duke, and Henry Currey.

But these came to nought and it was the early part of 1874 before the subject again came up. Dr Robertson was opposed to the idea of moving the baths to the hospital maintaining that by so doing the water would lose some of its medical efficacy and he continued in this opposition in correspondence with the duke and with George Drewry throughout the year. He conceded, however, that the hospital needs were for one natural bath and four hot baths and he proposed that the Charity Natural Bath be moved to the site of the Hot Baths where there was more room.

Remains of the Charity Natural Baths

The Duke of Devonshire argued successfully in a letter of December 23rd, that pumping up water to be used for hot baths would be no change to the present arrangements and that, if it should be found that the natural water was at all affected by being pumped to the hospital then arrangements might be made for a Charity Natural Bath in the lower land near or in the Crescent. Dr Robertson was still not minded to agree but the hospital committee proposed that the duke's suggestion, and his offer of £1500, be accepted. In the event a neat compromise was offered when an amended proposition was put to the committee by Mr Walton (a local bank manager) that the duke, through Mr Drewry, be asked if he would sell to the hospital a plot of land near the Local Board Office (on George Street) as a site for new baths, thus avoiding the need to pump up the water. Although this proposition was carried and the duke was written to in these terms, Dr Robertson continued to express his serious doubts about moving the baths from close to where the springs issued.

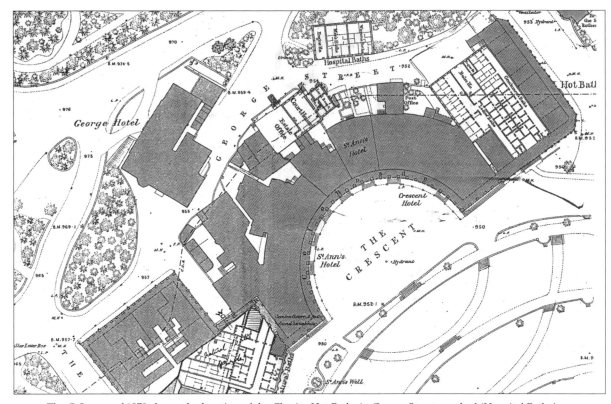

The O.S. map of 1879 shows the location of the Charity Hot Baths in George Street, marked 'Hospital Baths'.

This caused difficulties between the duke and the hospital committee. In January 1875 Mr Drewry asked Samuel Turner, his sub-agent, to put Robert Duke's plans for the new baths to the committee for approval. At the same time, he offered £1500 towards the cost of these baths and a supply of the mineral water from the unused overflow of the large gentleman's bath. Dr Robertson opposed the plan and suggested to the duke that not only were the medical men and subscribers to the hospital opposed to the removal of the Charity Baths from near to the springs, but also that this would affect the general well-being of the town. This attempt to put pressure upon the duke did not work. He replied withdrawing his offer of the George Street site and restating the view that the Charity Baths would not suffer by being sited at the hospital. Mr Walton again proposed that the duke's offer of finance and his permission for them to build the baths where they chose in the hospital should be accepted. It was carried unanimously - it seems Dr Robertson had to accept the inevitable.

Discussions now took place as to the most suitable site for these baths at the hospital. It was agreed that they should be erected at the south west boundary of the hospital grounds sunk to a level such that the water would flow naturally from the public baths to the new ones. Robert Duke was instructed to take out an estimate for their construction. However, the duke refused to allow the water to be fed by gravitation as proposed and the architect was asked to prepare an estimate for the building of the baths in the quadrangle of the hospital. The duke's agent was also putting pressure on the committee to vacate the present Charity Baths as soon as possible so that alterations to the public baths could proceed. The Devonshire Estate was clearly anxious to enlarge the facilities for paying visitors to the town as soon as possible.

In March of 1875 Robert Duke submitted plans for baths in the quadrangle of the hospital which entailed an 18,000 gallon tank being sunk 60 feet below the level of the hospital into which the water would flow by gravitation from the Natural Baths, and then be pumped up to the new baths. This was not considered a practical solution on the grounds of cost, and further discussions took place, on an alternative scheme put forward by the agent, George Drewry. In the event, the idea of siting the Charity Baths at the hospital was not pursued and by July the hospital committee approved plans by Robert Duke for new baths to be erected near to the Local Board office in George Street consisting of two hot baths for male patients, two hot baths for females and all necessary dressing and other rooms, together with an engine house and tank. Sketch plans for two natural baths with dressing boxes adjoining the existing Natural Baths were also approved and the architect was instructed to obtain estimates for completion.

This was a neat compromise in that the Charity Natural Bath would still be built on the site of the Natural Baths in the Crescent. Dr Robertson had succeeded in obtaining a solution which kept both baths on the level of the natural springs and the Charity Natural Bath close to the spring source. [42]

With the Charity Baths building underway no time was lost to expand the facilities in the Hot and Natural Baths and work was already progressing in October 1875. The trend towards provision of smaller private baths was continued in this refurbishment, with the Hot Baths being composed entirely of Private Baths. Separate corridors led to ranges of 10 private baths each for ladies and gentlemen. Each bath was equipped with a dressing room, douche equipment and shower bath, the individual baths were shallow and could be prepared to any temperature required.

The Natural Baths retained the three large Public Baths:

Firstly, the original Public Bath (formerly the Great Bath but much modified over the years) was now called the Two Shilling Bath. It measured twenty six by eighteen feet.

Secondly, the Gentlemen's No. 2 Bath, which had previously been called the Two Shilling Bath was now demoted to the One Shilling Bath. It measured twenty seven by fifteen feet.

Thirdly, the Ladies Public Bath.

In addition the Natural Baths now had four Private Baths for ladies and five for gentlemen each measuring eleven by five feet, together with the usual dressing rooms, douche apparatus and shower baths.

The work also included the relaying of the marble floors to the Gentlemen's Public Baths and the provision of additional douche apparatus. The main contractors for this work were J. Barnsley & Sons, with a firm called Haden & Co. carrying out the engineering work. The total contract, paid over the years 1875-7 was £7235 and Henry Currey was paid the usual 5% architect's fee.

The Victorian Resort

From the major rebuild of 1853 we have seen a continuing and not inconsiderable capital expenditure on the Hot and Natural Baths up to the mid 1870s, and we might expect to look for an extended period beyond this when the Buxton Estate would seek to capitalise on its investment. This is the case from 1877 to the end of the century when surplus between income and expenditure averaged £2700 per year. Apart from investment in new needle, vapour and massage baths, new waiting room, water tower and shops in 1887-88, outgoings were limited to operating expenses and modest maintenance costs, though at the Hot Baths the expenditure on coal was one of the highest of the operating costs and fairly regular payments were made for boiler maintenance and refurbishment.

A significant challenge to the Buxton natural mineral waters was the hydropathic movement

Malvern House Hydropathic on Hartington Road

which developed in Britain from the early 1840s and had a significant impact on water medicine, indeed, the medical profession as a whole. The term 'hydropathy' has a specific meaning. It refers to a method of cold water cure popularised by Vincent Priessnitz (1799-1851) of Graefenberg in Austrian Silesia. A degree of legend surrounds the origins of Priessnitz's methods. The son of a small farmer, he undertook no formal medical training yet his charismatic personality led to tales recounted by his followers. It was said that he had observed animals bathing and massaging their muscles in the springs flowing from the mountains above his home and had himself used a wet compress to cure a broken rib. The legends are repeated today. His cold water cure was based on the belief that health is the natural condition of the body and that only water can separate and carry off the foreign matter in the system causing illness. His procedures consisted largely of wet and dry packs to induce sweating, cold baths, and the douche or water spray. He combined this with drinking of pure water, exercise, outdoor work and diet in a regime which barred the use of any form of drugs.

Hydropathy was publicised in England by Captain R.T. Claridge, a contractor in asphalt, and the regime of hydropathy, or the 'water cure', became very popular receiving patronage from such notables as Charles Darwin, Edward Bulwer Lytton, Gladstone, Tennyson and Florence Nightingale at one or other of the many centres which flourished during the century.[43]

Hydropathy, which used ordinary water, opened up the establishment of hydropathic hotels which offered comfortable, sometimes luxurious, accommodation and a range of water treatments with diet and exercise regimes. There was a hydropathic hotel in Buxton by 1855. In April Mr Joseph Miller placed a large advertisement thanking those who had, for many years, patronised him as a shampooer and professor of the cold water cure and indicating that he had erected a commodious house at Hall Bank extensively fitted up as a hydro. This venture did not enjoy the success of hydros developing elsewhere at this time, such as Matlock, Malvern or Ilkley, even though Mr Miller ran his advertisement for some time and operated his business well into the 1870s.

It was not recognised as a significant medical facility in the town because members of the medical profession, led by Dr Robertson, placed such great faith in the medical efficacy of the Buxton mineral

Peak Hydropathic on Terrace Road

water and its natural gases. However, from the mid 1860s with the rise of the sanatorium movement, and with hydropathic establishments gradually becoming part of the medical establishment, hydros began to appear in the town. An Anglican minister, Revd. James Shore, came to Buxton to open the first of these, Malvern House Hydro, in 1866. He was a Devon man who had become involved in homoeopathic and hydropathic medicine at Smedley's Hydro and his own, Matlock House Hydro in Matlock.

The Malvern House became Buxton's most successful Hydro, with accommodation in 1867 for forty patients. By 1884 it could take 180 and by 1905 it had become the Buxton Hydro advertising 260 rooms. But in general the development of hydropathics in Buxton was both modest and slow. In 1870 Shore leased the Royal Hotel to run as a hydro, but this was short lived. In 1880 Dr Hyde formed a company to develop Buxton House on Terrace Road into the Peak Hydro to accommodate 150 guests.

The other establishments were smaller. The Corbar Hill Hydro, Manchester Road, was converted from the Clarendon private lodging house in the 1890s and there were two hydros on London Road, the Haddon House (later known as Haddon Grove and as Olivers), from 1883 and the Haddon Hall, built in 1903. After the First World War the Haddon Hall became known as the Haddon Hall and Oliver's Hydro. These hydros offered a range of water therapies and, latterly, electro and electro-water treatments as new techniques developed. Most were attended by qualified doctors and all combined their treatment with rest, bracing air and sensible diet.

The natural mineral water baths would always have the edge on these hydros, of course, but it was necessary for the Devonshire Buxton Estate to invest in the most up to date treatments and, no doubt, the medical specialists demanded this. In the years 1886 to 1888 the Estate extended the baths in each wing and provided new types of bath including needle, massage and vapour. In 1891 the Hot Baths consisted of 14 Private Baths for ladies and 10 for men and offered needle, Russian, vapour, massage and sitz treatments. The Natural Baths now had five Private Baths each for ladies and gentlemen as well as the Public Baths as before.

As the century progressed Buxton became increasingly popular as an inland medical resort such that by 1895 at least 4000 people were staying in town each week during the season requiring 24 hotels and more than 340 lodging houses to accommodate them. Attractions in town now included the Pavilion Gardens and Serpentine Walks, Corbar Woods, a theatre opened in 1899 and the Union Club for gentleman in 1886. Places of interest close by were Poole's Cavern, Lover's Leap and the Cat and Fiddle Inn. Contemporary writers give a feel for how life was in the town at this time:

'...After breakfast we set out for a stroll, intending to see some of the principle attractions of Buxton and its immediate environment. On reaching the area in front of the Crescent we were struck with the sudden change that appeared to have come over the place. An hour before everything was still and silent, now all is life and gaiety and fashion. Visitors were thronging from all points; the lame and the halt are slowly hobbling on towards the baths; others are indulging in their morning draught of mineral water, or aiding the effect by promenading to and fro along the Colonnade; others again are toiling up and down the steep Hall Bank, or sauntering along the walks of St Anne's Cliff; and here and there you may see a group of laughing merry-eyed youngsters in charge of a coquettish-looking nursemaid disporting themselves upon the turfy slopes. But the number of children is small comparatively, rheumatism and lumbago being among the ills that juvenile flesh is seldom heir to. Gay companies, in equally gay-looking equipages, start every now and then from the doors of St Anne's and the Old Hall to enjoy a forenoon airing; and people of less aristocratic class are bargaining with the

'March of the Men of Buxton' by Randolph Caldecott after his visit to Buxton in 1876.

owners of one-horse carriages for a drive to the Lover's Leap or the Cat and Fiddle, whilst in Spring Gardens, knots of eager pleasure seekers are gathering round the Peveril of the Peak bent upon a ride over the breezy moors to see the multifarious wonders that Castleton displays. Literature seems to be in favour with the stay-at-homes. The benches and rustic seats invitingly placed upon the gravelled walks are for the most part occupied by elderly gentlemen and their dames, many of whom are leisurely perusing the daily papers, or wading through the Advertiser's list of visitors and noting what new arrivals there have been since the Herald issued its long array of of names two or three days before...'[44]

The writer, James Croston, is referring to the local newspapers, *The Buxton Advertiser* and *Herald and Gazette of Fashion* whose practice was to list by name and accommodation the visitors to the town each week. For a description of the evening at Buxton we might turn to the one of the

'Off to Chatsworth' a cartoon
by W.G. Baxter c. 1880.

wonderful word pictures of
Edward Bradbury:

'...*Passing under our
window in a Bath-chair,
was Mr Blades, of
Sheffield, with flushed face.
Blades was very gross and
corpulent, with rich husky
voice; the pale man who pulled
him, consumptive and shrunken. Bath-chair men are generally pale and shrunken, and their
fares fat and ruddy. Blades smoked an old dry Manilla; chairman expectorated... A carriage
took us along the Duke's Drive, in the cool and fragrant evening air, with the sunset fire in the
sky. Afterwards we found ourselves again in the delightfully seductive grounds of the Pavilion,
where the orchestra was playing one of Godfrey's Schottisches, while icy and frigid duennas
worked themselves into a fierce heat with their fans, or stabbed reputations with their knitting
needles... At dusk there were fireworks. Quite a Crystal Palace display of pyrotechny... The
crowd, which was composed of gentility that would regard it as "awfully bad form, don't you
know" to applaud at a theatre, actually cried "oh!" in affected wonder at the rockets as they lit
up the dusky trees and flew upward... Sometimes a flying firework fell among the spectators, and
revealed young Manchester in a fit of amorous abstraction, stealing within his own the soft
white hand of Miss Stockport. Sometimes a sudden flash of light from a run-a-way squib, or a
cracker on the loose, showed somebody's sister allowing her brother's friend to span her waist
with his arm. At last the music died away; the fireworks faded, and spluttered and died; the cold*

'Pavilion Gardens' by W.G. Baxter.

moon blanched the trees and silvered the waterfall; and the bugle bade us retire. That hour after supper was not the least pleasant sensation of the day. Old-fashioned wax candles were lighted, and the curtains drawn across the windows...There was much to be seen and done during that short sojourn in the Derbyshire City of Hygieia...'[45]

The Haddon Hall Hydro shown here on a billhead six years after it was built.

New Pump Rooms

In 1882 the St Anne's Well Room situated in the Natural Baths, had become crowded and, in particular there were complaints of charity patients congregating in the colonnade near the well, to the annoyance of visitors. This problem was resolved when the hospital architect Robert R. Duke suggested that a Well Room for charity patients be built on George Street adjoining the new Charity Hot Baths. This was agreed to by the charity trustees and the well can be seen today still with the inscription 'Devonshire Hospital Drinking Well AD 1882 St Anne's Well Water Pump Room For Devonshire Hospital patients only'. The building now houses a large Victorian pump which formerly supplied the mineral water baths at the Devonshire Royal Hospital.[46]

    As the years went on the St Anne's Well became progressively more crowded and the idea of building a new Well or Pump Room was discussed. Various suggestions were made, including enlargement of the existing facility and sites to the north of the Square and where the present Opera House stands, but in the end a design for a new Pump Room, to be sited at the bottom of the slopes, was accepted. The architect was Henry Currey (the last substantial work he did in Buxton before his death in 1900) and the Pump Room was opened in 1894. The Pump Room provided elegant seating arrangements for those wishing to drink either the natural mineral or the chalybeate water. The town guide book of 1905 described the arrangements as '...*a polished counter, with a top of veined Italian marble, upon which are fixed five massive silvered fountains of suitable design and, through them the water flows continuously... whilst the well is open to visitors...* [47]

New provision for free access to the waters was made when the public double pump of 1855 was replaced in 1894 by a new pump which issued only the natural thermal water. It was sited close to the new Pump Room.

The Crescent showing the Pump Room being built. Work had begun by September 1892 and the builder's scaffolding seen to the right shows that this photograph was taken in the early stages of its construction.

Approaching the 20th Century

By 1896, in addition to the new Pump Room, the accommodation at the Baths had increased. At the Natural Baths were still the two Public Baths for gentlemen but now six Private Baths. The Ladies provision had not changed with one Public and 5 Private Baths. In the Hot Baths department there were 22 Private Baths, 2 less than in 1891.[48] It is possible that there had been a reduction in the Gentlemen's side to make way for new forms of bath treatment. At the turn of the century the range of treatments were described as follows:

'...*The Natural Baths, which have a stronger medicinal efficacy, are used only for the application of the waters at the natural temperature of the spring [82°F]. They consist of separate suites of baths for ladies and gentlemen, and each suite contains both private immersion and swimming baths. ...the swimming baths are supplied with a crane and lowering chair, and the baths are supplied with the usual douches. The Hot Baths, in which any quantity of the natural water carefully heated, is added to the naturally tepid water, in order to secure baths of any temperature that the circumstances of different cases may indicate. The Hot Baths have a lower degree of medicinal efficacy, estimated in the proportion of two-thirds - ie. three hot baths are estimated to be equal to two natural baths. The immersion baths are lined with marble and are entered by a short flight of steps with a protective rail. The water enters from apertures in the bottom and a half, three quarter or full bath can be given.*

The Needle Bath consists of circular metal tubes; each hoop of the tubing is perforated with numerous small holes, and when the pressure of water is turned on, emits a small jet or needle upon the bather. Combined with this are the ascending and descending and wave douches. The Buxton Massage and Douche Bath is a flat dish of copper coated with white metal, in which the patient reclines while treatment by douche and massage is applied. Vapour Baths - from evaporation of the natural water - may be used either as full bath, in which the patient is encased in a wooden box, with a round hole for the head in its movable lid; or in half bath, in which the patient is encased to the loins; or local bath, in which any joint may be treated with steam derived from the thermal water...'[49]

The main types of disease for which water treatment was being offered were: Gout; Rheumatism; Osteo and Rheumatoid Arthritis; some nervous diseases such as Neuralgia, Sciatica; Tropical diseases such as Malarial conditions; Heart Disease associated with Gout or Rheumatism; Digestive disorders; Skin diseases such as Gouty Eczema; Anaemia; Phthisis (Pulmonary Tuberculosis).

Though the use of water treatment is limited today to some forms of physiotherapy, in the 19th century it formed a most important branch of medicine, many different treatments and ways of using the water were developed and many different illnesses were treated, though it must be said that the medical practitioners lacked the diagnostic tools of today's doctors. Nevertheless, Buxton would have considered itself at the forefront of specialist water treatments by the end of the 19th century and many of the resident doctors wrote books on the subject, Dr Robertson's Guide to the use of the Buxton Mineral Waters running to more than 27 editions and still being reprinted after his death in 1897. As we shall see in the next chapter, Buxton continued to develop its water treatments, including the use of electricity in baths.

The Pump Room with open arches and the public pump of 1894

The Hot baths after the 1900 remodelling of the facade

The Hot baths after the 1909 addition of glass colonnading

CHAPTER FOUR

Changes at the Hot Baths

In 1900 the Hot Baths were remodelled both internally and externally. The shops which had faced the baths from 1863 were demolished and new shop accommodation was made available at the east side of the baths building, by this time known simply as the Colonnade. In place of the old shops were built new waiting and cooling rooms on either side of a central entrance hall from where the bath tickets were issued. The largest addition during this conversion was to the massage department which time housed on the first floor and could be reached by a staircase designed with a very easy gradient for those with walking difficulties. Others too infirm to use the stairs could take advantage of the newly installed hydraulic lift which was situated at the extreme end of the main corridor

Externally the iron and glass colonnading of 1854 was removed and a new classical stone frontage was erected made of tooled ashlar stone taken from the nearby Nithen quarry. The architect for the new frontage was W.R. Bryden of Buxton and the contractors for the whole of the work were J Parnell & Son of Rugby. Parnell later worked in Buxton on the building of the Empire Hotel in 1901-1903. The newly converted baths were opened in June 1901.[1]

The new stone frontage remained exposed to the elements until 1909 when glass and iron colonnading was erected using much of the old 1854 metalwork and incorporating coloured glass. The architects for the colonnade replacement were Bryden & Walton and the contractors, Messrs G J Bagshaw & Son. The Urban District Council took out a loan of £776 to pay for the replacement of the verandah though a total project cost of only £622 was reported in the *Buxton Advertiser*.[2]

Bathchair Men

During the early 1900s the bathchair was a common sight in the town, parked in ranks at the bottom of the Slopes in front of the Hot Baths. Other bathchair stands were opposite the Old Hall hotel, the Broad Walk end of Burlington road and on St John's road near the church. Bathchairs had been in use in Buxton since the early part of the 19th century when the town only had one such chair which was kept at the rear of the Hall hotel. The three-wheeled chairs were used to convey invalid patients to and from the baths and to various places throughout the town. The chairs protected the passengers from the elements with a folding front to cover the legs and a folding hood for total comfort. The bathchair man had no such luxuries and hauled his charge around the town, to and from the baths and, not infrequently, as far as the Cat & Fiddle Inn and the Goyt Valley.[3]

The satirist, Art Hacker, described them as the aristocracy of both the Higher and Lower town and suggested that they possessed all the Biblical attributes of the lilies of the field without much of their personal charm! He wryly observed the fate of the bath-chair men in the Pavilion Gardens which had no liquor licence:

> '...*The bath-chair men, too, hang miserably around till it shall please her ladyship to trundle home, and have ample reason, thirsty souls, to bemoan the waste of so much valuable time in a place where they have no license...*'[4]

The Baths become Public Property

The question of the public purchase of the baths from the Duke of Devonshire was first raised in April 1903 and by January of 1904 it had been agreed for the U.D.C. to purchase the baths for £25,000 plus an additional annual rent of £1000. The plan was beset by legal difficulties and it became necessary to promote a bill in Parliament. An objection was raised during the passage of the bill through the House of Lords on the grounds that their lordships could not agree to a perpetual annual Chief Rent. The idea of a chief rent was abandoned and the Natural and Hot Baths were eventually purchased for the sum of £55,000, the council taking out a loan for that amount. The loan was repayable over a period of 60 years with annual payments of £2431, making the total cost of the conveyance, including interest, £145,560.[5]

Work at the Pump Room

In 1910 Buxton U.D.C. appointed Frank Langley as Borough Surveyor and instructed him to submit a report on the general condition of the Natural Baths which had become somewhat neglected. The findings of this report resulted in a series of excavations at the baths which uncovered a new and abundant source of spring water in front of the Natural Baths. This was at such a level as to allow the nearby pump room to be supplied with gravity fed water from this source thus removing the need for pumping apparatus to discharge water at the serving counter.

In 1912 work took place to the plans of Langley for major structural changes at the Pump Room. In order to increase the internal floor area the open arcading on the front of the building which had existed since its construction in 1893/4 was enclosed. A well chamber was built at the rear which contained a sunken marble basin into which the mineral water flowed through holes in its base. The main contractors for the work were largely local people. Robinson Bros of Buxton supplied masons & bricklayers, Edward Brown supplied the joinery, J. Brocklehurst carried out the plastering and the new plumbing was installed by E. Broomhead. Much new marble was introduced during this conversion which was supplied and fitted by the Manchester firm of J & H Patteson.

The enlarged Pump Room was reopened to the public on 1st July 1912 by the Duke of Devonshire. After the conversions it was felt that it was no longer strictly accurate to call the building a pump room and it was therefore renamed St Anne's Well. On completion the building had two entrances, one at each end which soon became a source of difficulty for the local council since they now had to pay the wages of two, instead of one ticket attendant. An entrance charge was made at the well which included as many glasses of water as the customer desired. The cost of the conversions was in the region of £2,875 which was raised as a loan by the UDC.[6]

The converted pump room was very elegantly decorated internally with oak panelled walls and stained glass windows which remain today. Two female assistants were employed at the marble pool, one ladling the water from the pool with a glass in a holder on the end of a long metal pole. The other assistant took the glass from the holder and passed the full glass to the customer who waited at the other side of the marble balustrading surrounding the pool.

Treatments at the Baths

By 1909 the Buxton Baths were advertising a wide variety of treatments. At the Natural Baths there remained separate swimming baths for ladies and gentlemen. Doctors Armstrong & Harburn, who were practising in Buxton in the early 20th century, recommended an immersion in the swimming baths of between 5 and 12 minutes and patients were encouraged to move their limbs as much as possible whilst in the bath to liberate the gases contained in the water. The douche was often used in conjunction with a visit to the bath and a recommended bath of 8 minutes duration would consist of a 4 minute swim, a 2 minute douche followed by a further 2 minute swim.[7]

In addition to the Buxton Douche Massage, the vapour baths and the needle baths, all mentioned in the previous chapter, the Hot Baths also offered a multitude of ways to apply water to the body: the Sitz bath was a shallow bath, big enough for only one person to immerse trunk & thighs: the Plombiere Douche (spa water enema, first introduced in the French town of Plombiere) was in much demand; and the Aix & Vichy douches (similar to the Buxton Douche Massage). In the Aix douche the patient sat upright in a chair as one or two attendants performed massage whilst running streams of hot water over the body. The Vichy massage differed in that the patient reclined in a bath on a hot water mattress and massage was applied with the hot water flowing over the body.[8]

Relaxation away from the Baths

Although the water treatment took up some of the time of the health seeker there remained substantial parts of the day and evening which could be used for the purposes of entertainment. Those interested in sport could visit the Buxton Football Club at the Silverlands ground, or play golf on either of the town's well laid out courses in Fairfield and Burbage. During the summer months cricket was played on the Cricket ground in the Park. The dramatic arts could be seen at the Entertainment Stage of 1889 on St John's Road, later known as the New Theatre. The magnificent Opera House was opened in 1903 and took over the theatre provision, from then on hosting many famous actors and actresses over time: Alec Guinness, Stewart Granger, Anthony Quayle and Dame Sybil Thorndike to name but a few. The old theatre was fitted with projection equipment, changed its name to the Hippodrome and showed silent films. Further cinema facilities were provided in Spring Gardens in 1916 with the erection of the glass colonnaded Picture House.[9]

The official handbook of 1921 described the Pavilion Gardens with its many acres of beautifully laid-out grounds, recognised to be the finest in the country. There the visitor could listen to orchestral concerts in the pavilion or on the terrace. In the afternoon 'The's Dansants' (tea dances) were given

Hot baths Colonnade in 1910.

during the winter season and musical teas in the summer. Sports enthusiasts could play tennis, croquet

Bathchairman on Broad Walk

Interior of St Anne's Well after 1912 conversions

Ticket office at the Hot baths early 20th century.　　　Entrance to the Hot baths early 20th century.

and bowls or go boating. In the winter roller-skating, ice-skating and curling were indulged in. An up-to-date cafe opened all the year round. The visitor was also pointed in the direction of The Slopes (or St Anne's Cliff), the Serpentine Walks, Grinlow Woods and Corbar Crags for good views of the town. By 1925 the Burbage Golf Club had been transferred to the newly opened Cavendish Golf Links, laid out by noted course designer, Dr Alister Mackenzie, and opened in April.[10]

Comfort and style at the Hot and Natural Baths

Although it was intended to modernise and extend the Natural Baths in 1912, financial and other considerations caused the council to concentrate their efforts on improvements at the Hot Baths. - at the time more treatments were dispensed and the greatest revenue came from these. Frank Langley designed a series of changes which seem to have been largely decorative, involving extensive use of wall tiling and the installation of much marble. The modernisation work was completed in time for the 1913 season at a cost of £6,000.

The plans for a major upgrading at the Natural Baths, which had been prepared by Langley, had been subjected to much delay but were finally approved in 1914. The intervention of World War I further delayed the implementation of the scheme. During the following years a number of amended plans were submitted to the council for consideration and it was not until 1922, following a loan of £19,500 from the Ministry of Health, that work on the conversions began.

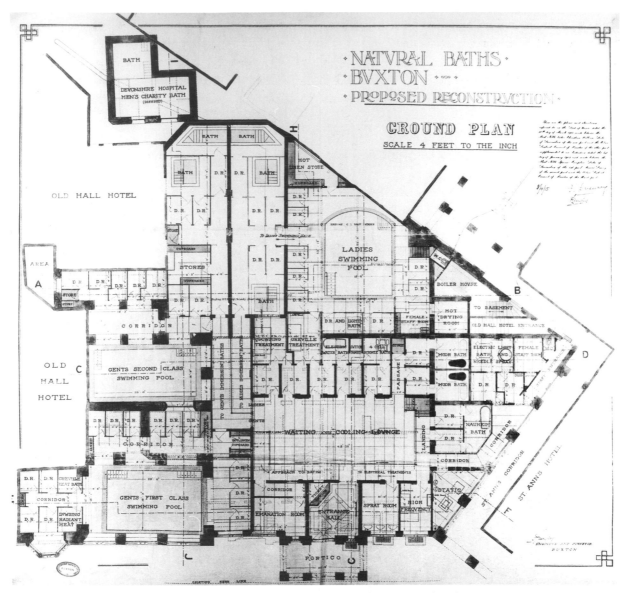

Langley's 1915 plan for conversions at the Natural Baths

We have been able to identify two plans which relate to this work, one dating to April 1915, the other to December 1921.[11] Using these plans for guidance we can see that new types of baths and new plunge baths were built during this reconstruction together with rooms to house the new electrical treatments within the building. The room housing the Gentlemens' first class bath was extended and the floor of the bath was paved with Sicilian marble slabs which were perforated to allow the gas which is naturally released from the spring to rise through the water.

The three large swimming pools (Gents 1st class, Gents 2nd class and the Ladies) were renovated but remained largely unchanged from their layout in 1853. Adjacent to the Gentlemen's Second Class Bath a new connection was made to the first floor of the Old Hall Hotel thus providing a covered passage from the hotel to the baths. The south facade of the baths was completely remodelled in the same style and materials as used by Currey in 1853. The facade was raised, the balustrading altered and the stonework in the piers redesigned.

Changes were made to the ticket office and entrance hall and the work also included the modelling of the present entrance to the baths from the road side using Darley Dale Ashlar stone. The floors of the public rooms were paved in black and white marble and the walls were lined with Carrara Arni Vein marble and Kerry red marble bands. The whole building was re-roofed, replacing the earlier slated ridge and furrow roof. The main contractor for the work was J. Ridyard and son of Ashton-under-Lyne.

The newly reconstructed baths were opened in May 1924 by the President of the Royal College of Physicians, Sir Humphrey Rolleston.

In addition to the three large pools there were now 3 Ladies and 3 Gents private immersion baths. A number of small new rooms were set aside for the exclusive dispensing of one particular treatment including the Electric Water Bath, three Moor Baths, a Nauheim Bath, Static and High Frequency Rooms and two Greville Treatment Rooms. The Greville treatment involved the blowing of super heated air on to the affected part of the body prior to immersion in a warm bath. The Greville equipment had been purchased in 1920 using a loan of £700.

The use of electricity in conjunction with the water treatment had gradually become more popular and by the 1920s had reached its peak. The combination of water and electrical current may sound rather frightening but many variants of such treatments were on offer at the Natural Baths. There were the Electro-water bath, the four-cell Schnee bath, the D'Arsonval High Frequency and the Dowsing Radiant Light & Heat Treatment. Popular, perhaps for its novelty value was the Electric Light Bath which consisted of a wardrobe like arrangement which was fitted with electric light bulbs on its inner surfaces. The patient stood in the middle of this chamber and in some cases was sprayed with a water douche.[12]

Electro-vibratory massage was available and Fango mud treatments were given using mud specially imported

Gents Pool 1924 after major refurbishment of the Baths

Ladies Pool 1924 after major refurbishment of the Baths

from Fango, Italy. A room at the front of the Natural Baths building housed the Nauheim Bath which used effervescent salt water as introduced from the German spa of Bad Nauheim. Guide books of 1924 feature a new addition to the treatment list, the Whirlpool Bath, which was specially adapted for limbs affected by gunshot wounds, cases of which would not have been unusual given the recent 1914-18 war.

The Natural Baths offered the popular Peat or Moor baths which were housed in three bathing cubicles. Each cubicle housed a small bath-shaped hole in a raised slab of marble. The hole looked down into the baths basement where specially constructed peat trucks ran on two foot gauge rails. The trucks when filled with their peat mixture were trundled into position under the hole in the marble slab and a sliding door was closed behind it. The naked patient, lowered into the truck, lay immersed up to the neck for about twenty minutes. A careful eye was kept on the peat bather by the bath attendant because some could not cope with the whole treatment and needed to be helped from the bath early. The patient was then hosed down with a fine needle spray in the small bath and wrapped in hot towels for a further twenty minutes. When the cubicle was finally vacated the bath attendant rang a bell and the boilerman wheeled back the truck into the cellar and disposed of the used peat through an earthenware pipe which drained into a culvert leading to the river Wye. The trucks and rails remain under the baths and are still in remarkably good condition.

The baths were prepared by the boilerman which took some time and it was thus necessary to make an appointment for a moor bath. He put a quantity of peat into the truck and added

Above: Patient receiving water douche after peat treatment
Right: Patient receiving a Peat Bath
Below:
Remains of a peat truck under the Natural Bath

water which was stirred using a paddle. Steam was then introduced into the mixture, raising the temperature to anything from 90°F to 105°F (32-40°C). The water used in the peat mixture was originally taken from the chalybeate source in the belief that its high iron content mixed with the acidic peat enhanced the efficacy of the treatment. By 1953 the iron pipes which were used to carry the chalybeate water had become badly corroded which compromised the pureness of supply and mineral or ordinary tap water was used instead. Peat for these baths was taken from the moors on the south eastern side of the Cat & Fiddle road. The peat was stored in a building at Burbage reservoir until needed when it was brought by lorry to the rear of the baths and tipped into the cellar.[13]

On Well Dressing Saturday in 1952, the Duchess of Devonshire was treated to a peat bath just before the Natural Baths closed for the day. The Duke of Devonshire was mayor that year and both were in the town for the festivities. The Duchess remembers the experience vividly. With her customary wit she summed it up as being: '...*like stepping down into a bath filled with hot cow pats...*'[14]

Charity Baths now at the Devonshire Hospital

As we have seen in the previous chapter, Buxton's foremost water physician, Dr W.H. Robertson, had argued strenuously that the water would lose its healing properties if it were moved too far from its source. This resulted in the compromise solution to site the Charity Baths of 1876 in George street and behind the Old Hall Hotel. Dr Robertson died in 1897 and with him the strongly held reservations against siting the baths at a distance from the water source. His successors held different views for in 1914 new baths were built on ground adjoining the south front of the Devonshire Hospital. The baths were in regular use by the end of the year. and were designed by the local architectural practice of Bryden and Walton.[15]

This meant that the patients of the Bath Charity no longer had to make the journey from the hospital to the charity baths on George Street and at the rear of the Old Hall Hotel which, for the more severely infirm, would have been an arduous task. The new baths were fed with the natural mineral water from the 1882 drinking well building on George Street, by way of a large and powerful pump which was probably installed as part of the 1914 hospital baths project. Due to the increased amount of steam required to heat the new baths and the poor state of the existing boiler the scheme also included the building of a new boiler house, new boilers and an upgrade of the hospital's heating system. The total cost of the project was £8551.

The patients now had in-house baths at the hospital which could be reached by a sloping walkway from the dome floor into a corridor which led through to a porch and door on the south front. The baths on either side of the corridor were symmetrical; men's to the west side, women's to the east, each set of baths containing Plombiere, immersion, massage, douching and vapour baths together with dressing boxes and a waiting area.[16] The old Charity Hot and Natural Baths were closed but the Drinking Well Room remained in use housing the gravity pump which still exists in the building today.

The Buxton Clinic

Affluent health seekers continued to be treated at the Hot and Natural Baths and the poor continued to receive treatment at the Devonshire Hospital through the Bath Charity. It seems, however, that by the 1930s it was felt that there was a niche in the market to provide bathing facilities for the so called 'middle class patient with limited means'. This led to the formation of a private company known as the Buxton Clinic Ltd under the chairmanship of Mr W. F. Wrigley. The Buxton Clinic was situated in the east wing of the Crescent and was officially opened by Lord Horder (physician to the then Prince of Wales) on April 26th 1935.

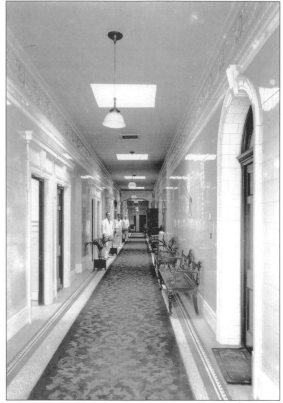

Gentlemen's corridor, Hot Baths, 1935

Ladies' corridor, Hot
Baths, c. 1920

Buxton Clinic was in
the Eastern Pavilion
of The Crescent.

Patients from the clinic received their treatment at the adjacent Hot Baths and had the use of lounges, writing rooms, billiards and a library. Social functions were held at the clinic and the patients' dining room was housed in the assembly room on the first floor of the building. Residents were also granted free entry into the Pavilion Gardens during their period of treatment. In 1935 the Clinic was advertising accommodation for 110 patients, '... *At a cost within the means of the middle classes...*'

The price of one week's treatment at the clinic ranged from 4 to 6 guineas and the recommended period of treatment was three weeks. In April 1938 the Clinic completed a scheme of extension, adding two floors to the establishment.[17] Following the introduction of the NHS the Buxton Clinic was annexed to the Devonshire Royal Hospital and 'amenity' beds were provided in single or two and three-bedded rooms for a small payment under the Health Service. This continued until June 1963 when the annex closed for treatments but it was used until 1966 as a geriatric unit.

Further initiatives in Water Treatment

The Buxton Corporation Accounts of December 1937 show that the baths and wells undertaking was £1000 down on the previous year. Working expenditure on both sets of baths rose from £6838 to £7534 but income from treatments fell from £6139 to £5800 and after the addition of £102 miscellaneous income the net trading deficiency was £1452. It is interesting to compare this loss with the healthy trading figures at the baths during the height of their popularity, as recorded in chapter three, where we have seen the Natural & Hot Baths taking an average annual net profit of £4,000 in the 1870s. No lowering of standards was allowed, however, and a visit from the British Health Resorts Association in 1938 resulted in a very satisfactory report on Buxton's bathing facilities.

Despite the falling income from the baths discussions were underway in 1937 to pursue the notion of a centre of excellence at Buxton. The Buxton Co-ordinating Committee, a body consisting of the three main organisations in the town dealing with rheumatic complaints, namely, the Devonshire Royal Hospital, the Natural and Thermal Baths and the Buxton Clinic, took up the idea with the Empire Rheumatism Council. The Devonshire Royal Hospital also issued a booklet seeking donations for ambitious enlargements of facilities. Neither of these initiatives succeeded but the thinking was carried through into the following decade.[18]

From the mid 1940s onwards the government was well advanced in its plans for the new National Health Service which was due to be launched in 1948. The water authorities of the town were aware of the big changes to come and perhaps because of this, and their earlier thinking, representatives of the water treatment establishments took the opportunity to announce plans for a significant expansion of services. The plan, submitted in 1947 by the Buxton Co-ordinating Committee, proposed setting up a 'Rheumatism Centre' within the framework of the National Health Service Act, using the three institutions to provide a comprehensive range of treatments for sufferers of rheumatic conditions. It was also intended to incorporate the plans made in 1945 to extend the Devonshire Royal Hospital (DRH) and increase the number of beds at the Buxton Clinic from 75 to 150, bringing the total numbers up to over 800.[19]

This was by any reckoning, an ambitious plan and its proponents were very aware of the cost implications of the project and the many difficulties they would encounter during its development. In the event the Rheumatism Centre never got off the drawing board, due to the government's view that once the hospital had been absorbed into the National Health Service the new methods of treatment on offer rendered such regional centres unnecessary.

Developments at the Natural Baths

In the mid 20th century at least one major redesign of the Natural Baths took place as may be seen by comparing the Langley changes of 1924 with plans of the layout in 1950. But the later plans show, graphically, the reduction in popularity of the electrical treatments which had been so sought after in the early part of the century. Gone were the Greville rooms, the Electric Light Baths, the Dowsing Radiant Heat rooms and the 4 cell Schnee Baths.[20] The introduction of the National Health Service in 1948 did not help the fortunes of the baths. It had been hoped that the new NHS would take over spa establishments throughout the country, thus giving the Buxton baths a sound financial footing. In the event spas were excluded from the NHS, but the Borough Council won a minor concession from the government which allowed for spa treatment to be financed by the NHS at the Devonshire Royal Hospital if such treatment was prescribed by a doctor.

Whilst traditional bathing medicine declined at the Natural Baths, a range of physiotherapy treatments were developed. A guide book of 1946 showed three pools in use for remedial exercises and swimming under trained supervision. Also on offer were aeration, immersion and peat baths, and ultra violet and paraffin wax treatments. In the 1950s the Hubbard Tank, artificial sunlight and diathermy were available and plans of about this time include an additional Moor bath which fits in with the generally held opinion that the Peat or Moor bath had a lingering popularity and was one of the last of the treatments to be phased out.

The Hot Baths

As we know, the Hot Baths used the natural mineral water which was heated to various temperatures depending on the nature of the treatment. The natural water was piped from the Natural Baths, across the front of the Crescent into a long tank under the road in front of the Hot Baths facade. From there it was piped to two tanks at the rear of the building and then to two further tanks in the water tower in the centre of the building. There were two boilers housed in the baths which were kept in constant use during the day and the boilerman was kept busy attending the boilers and mixing peat for baths and packs. The boilerman started his day at 7.00 am so that the water could be heated in time for the arrival of the patients and he also worked in the evenings and on Sundays, after the baths were closed, to stoke the boilers. One of the two boilers was a Cornish type with a vertical boiler and the other was a Lancashire boiler which had two horizontal barrels. The coke to power the boilers came from the Buxton Gasworks until 1962 when these gasworks closed and coke was brought from Chesterfield.

The two main corridors into the baths, one for men, the other for women led deep into the baths complex from separate entrances at the front of the building. At the end of the corridors was the deep pool, 10 feet square and 6 feet deep, the largest bath in the establishment. It was lined with marble slabs and had marble steps leading down into the water. Patients could either sit on these steps to exercise their limbs or if they were more mobile they could exercise in the deep water. The pool was also equipped with a douche hose should a patient require an underwater massage.

Mrs Freda Rennicks began work at the deep pool in 1953 and was regularly called upon to lower the more infirm patients into the baths by use of a wooden wheelchair which was positioned at the bath side. Both chair and patient were lowered into the water using a winch fixed at the side of the bath. Treatment in the deep pool, for both men and women, was given by the hydrotherapists, Jimmy Needham and Jack Kay. Each treatment session lasted for 20 minutes which necessitated the bathing assistants spending lengthy periods in the water and to prevent weariness from continuous immersion, they worked in two hour shifts.

A large amount of linen was used at the baths in the shape of towels, peat sheets, uniforms, and a laundry was on site to deal with it. This laundry was situated in the Hot Baths complex but dealt with the washing from the Natural Baths and St Anne's Well together with its own. Hannah Nall was the sole washerwoman and she used an industrial washing machine. After the Charity Hot Baths in George Street became redundant in 1914, part of the building was used as public wash baths which were frequented by those townspeople whose house did not have a bathroom. The hot water for the baths was provided by the boilerman at the Hot Baths and a bath, in the 1940s, cost 6d. In 1947 four new public wash baths were built beside the Hot Baths boilerhouse.

In 1946 equipment was purchased for giving wax treatment to patients who had rheumatism in their hands or wrists. The patients put their hands into a small bath of heated wax for a few seconds, When they removed it the hand was coated with a thin layer of wax. This process was repeated until the hand was encased in many layers of wax. The patient had to be careful not to move their hand or fingers otherwise the wax would crack and the treatment would not be as effective. When the treatment was finished, the wax could be sterilised and used again. Wax treatment had been used as early as 1921 at Buxton Baths and the Devonshire Royal Hospital and may have developed out of the treatment during the Great War.

Alternative Uses for the Natural Baths

Treatments at the Natural Baths finished in January 1954 and all the treatments and staff were moved to the Hot Baths. The closure coincided with the retirement of several members of staff of many years standing. Joe Brunt, whose speciality was the Buxton Douche, had worked in the treatment establishments for 50 years. Two years earlier his two sisters Jessie and Alice had retired from the spa after 45 and 44 years respectively. Miss Manly, Mrs Birch and Mary Fry also retired at the closure and it is hardly surprising that the loss of so many experienced people caused problems for the manager, Mr R A Lockwood. Temporary staff had to be engaged and one of the 'old brigade', Alf Martin, came back to help out. Mr Martin had retired for the first time in 1948 at the age of 71. He had worked at the Baths for 32 years in two separate stints. He returned in 1955 and gave electrical treatment and worked in the deep pool, finally retiring in 1959, aged 80.

In 1958 some of the aeration baths were concreted over in order to make a level surface for a changing room. This left the three large pools in the building available for swimmers and thus it became the town's public swimming baths. Many of the town's residents will remember these baths, particularly the Gentlemens' first class bath which was built over the main thermal spring and was floored with perforated slabs which allowed the water and bubbles of gas to enter the pool. The water when seen in quantity in a pool of that size showed its natural pale blue colouring. The second of the pools, the Gentlemens' second class bath was less popular with swimmers because of its lack of natural lighting but the Ladies bath, with its bright lighting from the glass roof was a pleasant, if small bath.

Even though the baths were given over to the use of swimmers it was still believed that immersion in the thermal water should be subject to a time limit as the waters were apt to induce tiredness. When the bather handed in their clothes for safe keeping, draped on a metal frame designed for the purpose, a note was taken of the number and time of entering the bath. After the allotted time the attendant called out the number at the poolside and the bather was obliged to get out and get dressed.

After 1961 the time allowed was increased to 30 minutes.[21]

As the popularity of therapeutic bathing continued to diminish new uses were found for the facilities. In the 1950s the oak panelled cooling room was hired out to various private organisations including the Old Peoples Welfare Coordinating Committee, the Professional Women's Club, the Gospel Hall and the Fencing club in order to raise income. The minutes of the Baths and Wells Committee of 1950 record an agreement to give the exclusive use of the Gentlemen's second class pool to the Divisional Education Committee to provide swimming instruction for school children. In June 1959 the Gentlemen's first class bath was hired by Jehovah's witnesses for the purpose of a mass baptism.[22]

The Hot Baths in the 1950s

In the 1950s the Hot Baths could still offer a large range of treatments and the complex contained 13 immersion pools for ladies and 6 for gentlemen, 3 vapour baths for ladies and 4 for gentlemen together with separate rooms for treatments such as the Plombière Douche, the Aix Douche, Buxton Douche Massage, peat packs, liver packs and various heat treatments. Each treatment was separately priced and inclusive tickets for two or three weeks of treatment could be bought. Plans dating to 22 January 1952 suggest that alteration and reconstruction of the roof of the ladies Douche Massage Department on the first floor of the Hot Baths may have been carried out at that time or was certainly contemplated.[23]

Amongst the famous visitors in the 1950s was Archbishop Makarios of Cyprus. The orchestral conductor, Sir Thomas Beecham took an entire suite at the Palace Hotel and brought his own grand piano with him. The earlier idea of limiting treatment in the Buxton water seems to have carried

Masseur Alf Martin at the Buxton Douche Bath.

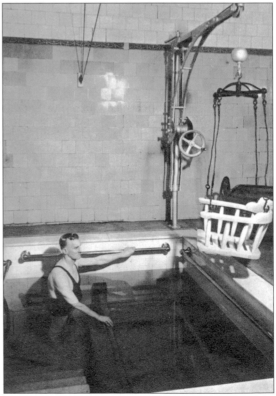

Right: Immersion Bath with crane.

through to this time because a feature of a course of treatment was that wet and dry days alternated. On wet days, a patient would have an immersion bath or a peat bath and on a dry day they would have electrical treatment or a massage. On Sir Thomas's dry days, the head masseur, Joe Fearn would treat him in his hotel suite. When the manager, Mr Lockwood left in 1959, Mr Fearn took over the post until the closure of the Hot Baths in 1963. Mr Fearn continued to operate after the closure, based in a part of the Natural Baths complex, using some of the redundant electrical equipment and with this he visited hotels and nursing homes in the town giving treatment to residents and visitors in their own rooms. In the 1950s football teams were regular visitors to the Hot Baths. As well as the two Manchester teams, Nottingham Forest, Notts County, both Sheffield teams, Newcastle United, Blackpool, Leicester City, Cardiff City, Everton, Middlesbrough and Southampton all came. They would typically stay at the Palace Hotel for a couple of days and take tonic aeration baths and Buxton Douche Baths to tone them up for their matches. Some players had injuries which were helped by Buxton treatment.[24]

Closure of the Hot Baths

Despite the range of treatments on offer at the Hot Baths patient numbers declined from the mid 1950's and representations were made to the Regional Hospital Board expressing concern over the decreasing use of the Hot Baths by the NHS. The Devonshire Royal Hospital had its own baths suite which was modified by the introduction of a new deep hydrotherapy pool in 1952, further extended in 1957. In 1962 the Lancashire boiler developed a serious fault and was condemned, leaving only the Cornish boiler. When this boiler had to be descaled a few months later no wet treatments were performed for a period of eight days.[25]

The change of use of the east wing annex of the Crescent from a water treatment clinic to a geriatric unit had an immediate and dramatic effect at the baths. This is borne out by a report in June 1963 from the baths manager to the Bath and Wells Committee stating that there had been a sudden drop in the number of treatments given at the baths from 454 patients in one week to only 102 the following week. Despite the immediate dismissal of 3 hydrotherapy assistants, one receptionist, a boilerman and a

Ladies Natural Bath c. 1920

cleaner the Hot baths were obviously no longer viable and closed on 30 September 1963. One of the bath attendants at the Hot Baths, Mary Hargreaves, who had administered Peat, Aeration baths and Buxton Douch Massages for thirty years said of the closure, '...*The water is God's gift to the town and it is being thrown away...*'

Hydrotherapy continued, however, at the Devonshire Royal Hospital where a further pool was installed in 1979-80 to provide additional facilities for the head injuries ward.

Closure of the Natural Baths

The Natural Baths were closed for three months beginning in May 1957 in order to install new chlorinating apparatus and fit scum channels. In 1959 dry rot was found in the building and the baths closed on February 9th of that year. Although the closure of the baths was probably intended to be permanent, the public pressure for swimming facilities appeared to persuade the council to reopen the the baths on a temporary basis in 1961. Despite this temporary intention the baths remained in use as public swimming baths throughout the 1960s but were closed regularly for short periods for essential repairs. A new public swimming bath at the Pavilion Gardens was commenced in 1969 by the architectural practice of J. Poulson but completed by Booth, Hancock & Johnson of Pontefract. It was opened by Princess Anne in November 1972 at which time the Natural Baths were closed.

Over time the Natural Baths building has remained empty and concern has been expressed about its likely rapid deterioration. However, English Heritage together with the High Peak Borough Council have ensured that the baths are kept wind and weather tight.

It is ironic that the town should have invested in a 60 year mortgage to buy the baths in 1904 only to see them close a year prior to the loan being repaid.

The Natural Baths building today houses the Tourist Information Centre, the main part of which is situated in the former oak panelled Cooling Room. Through a window at the centre can still be seen the remains of the Great or Gentlemen's first class bath. It has been greatly reduced in size and is now covered by perspex housing to prevent contamination. It is from this point - the main spring - that water is taken for bottling purposes, and to supply St Anne's public well. The outflow feeds an underground chamber and the old 'Gentlemans Second-Class Bath' from where

Remodelled lounge at the Natural Baths 1924.
It is now the Tourist Information Centre

the spa water swimming pool at the Pavilion Gardens and the small fountain in front of the Crescent are fed. This secondary source also formerly fed the hydrotherapy pools at the Devonshire Royal Hospital via a pump in George Street. The remaining water is diverted into the river Wye.

New Use for the Hot Baths

The 1909 glass and iron colonnading fronting the Hot Baths was taken down in the 1960s due to its unsafe condition but the colonnading around the corner, on the east side of the building remained and was restored by the Borough Council in 1975. Similarly the colonnading across the road fronting the Grove Hotel and the west end of Spring Gardens remains and has been restored in recent years. In 1985/6 the Hot Baths building, which had deteriorated markedly after its closure, was converted into a shopping centre, the 'Cavendish Arcade', at a cost of £598,000. The architect for the project was Derek Latham and the contractors were the Chapel en le Frith building company, G D Rogers. Although the

Hot Baths during conversion in 1985

baths were removed during this conversion, effort was made to preserve part of the baths heritage with a small plunge bath (referred to as a Deep Pool on a 1963 plan) restored within the complex and by retaining the original wall tiling and a further, smaller, bath which can be seen under a metal grating inside one of the shops. The completed arcade was topped with a 3,000 square feet barrel-vaulted, stained glass roof designed by the artist Brian Clarke at an additional cost of £100,000.[26] In 2002 refurbishment by the architect Colin Mackenzie of David Coles Architects included prominent historical interpretation boards explaining the history of the baths.

Later History of St Anne's Well

The 1894 free public pump adjacent to St Anne's Well was replaced in 1940 by the present pump. Inscribed 'A well of living waters' it was dedicated to Emilie Dorothy Bounds, Councillor of the Borough, by her husband and daughter.

There are several photographs in existence dating to the 1930s of the water being served at St Anne's Well, by young women standing by the well. They were twins, called Emma and Beatrice, who had come from Nottingham with their father when he had been transferred to Buxton to run the goods department of the London, Midland and Scottish Railway. The two girls wanted to find a job where they could work together and by sheer chance they heard that two people were needed at the Pump Room. They were both taken on and began their day at 7.45am and finished at 7.00pm. Despite the hours, they spent a happy time there until Emma left to get married.

Emm and Bee, as they were more commonly known, served the water together. Bee scooped up the water from the well chamber in a glass fixed to a holder on the end of a long wand and swung the whole to Emm in one elegant movement. without the glass falling out of the holder. Emm would remove the glass and wipe it dry before handing it to the waiting customer. It was about 8 feet from the well surface to the top of the balustrade and Emm had to stand on a step so that she could reach up high enough. Some patients took the water 3 times a day and over the 3 weeks of their course of treatment they got to know Emm and Bee quite well.

By the 1950s only one assistant was employed at the well in an effort to reduce costs. To achieve this a swan neck pipe was installed over the pool which poured the thermal water into the pool from above unlike the previous arrangement when the pool had been filled from below. Since the glasses could be filled directly from this pipe only one assistant was required. Water could still be drawn from the dispensing pool at the well in the 1970s when the building housed the Tourist Information Centre but access to the pool was terminated when the Micrarium took over the premises in the early 1980s.

Emma and Beatrice, known as 'Em and Bee' dispensing water at St Anne's

The Micrarium used a unique display technique to show the microscopic world of animal and plant life through a selection of projection microscopes. Due to the retirement of the proprietor the Micrarium closed in 1996. The building is presently used on a seasonal basis as a gallery for local artists where the dispensing well is once again on show to the public and can often be seen full of mineral water fed in original fashion through holes in its bottom.

Buxton Water in Bottles

Buxton might reasonably claim to be the first spa to have its natural mineral water transported some distance in receptacles for drinking. So full of praise for Buxton water was the Earl of Leicester that, shortly after his return to court in July 1577, the Queen asked him to have sent to her a tun of the water in hogsheads which were to be thoroughly seasoned with the water beforehand. The water was sent but, it seems, Elizabeth was not disposed to drink any of it. [27]

The bottling of the water is, however, a much later innovation. In the early part of the 20th century the chalybeate and natural mineral water were offered for sale in bottles. In 1909 the chalybeate could be bought for 6d. a bottle or 5s. 6d. per dozen only from the Baths and Pump Room. By 1912 both the chalybeate and natural mineral water were available in bottles from St Anne's Well and Chalybeate Spring.[28] Sales of the bottled water by the Buxton Corporation continued until 1948 when the Apollinaris Company were able to market the water nationally. In June 1955 the premises were taken over by Schweppes, and then again in November 1955 by the local firm, Tebbs Mineral Water Company who not only bottled the spring water but also used the plant for the bottling of soft drinks and beer. The firm of H.O. Tebb was established to manufacture table waters in the late 19th century.

RETAIL PRICE LIST

BUXTON
(Source—St. Ann)

TABLE WATER
Sparkling or Still

Price per Dozen.		Price per Dozen.	
Baby (4 oz.) -	**4/-**	Medium (11 oz.) -	**7/6**
Small (7 oz.) -	**5/6**	Large (24 oz.) -	**11/-**

When ordered direct from the Source, the Buxton Corporation pays Carriage on all orders of 6 doz. and upwards to any part of the United Kingdom.

Allowance on sound returned bottles, per dozen :

Baby	...	**1/-**	Medium	...	**1/6**
Small	...	**1/6**	Large	...	**2/-**

Cases 4/- extra and allowed on Sound Return.
THE LARGE BOTTLES OF STILL WATER ARE SPECIALLY RECOMMENDED TO THOSE PATIENTS WHO WISH TO SUPPLEMENT THE TREATMENT ON RETURNING HOME.

ORDER FORM.

Please send me a consignment of "Buxton Natural Spring" as under :

	Per Dozen.	Number Required.
Baby (4 oz.)	4/-	
Small (7 oz. Splits)	5/6	
Medium (11 oz.)	7/6	
Large (24 oz.)	11/-	

State whether "Sparkling" or "Still"

This order can be sent or handed to your Wine Merchant, Grocer, Pharmacist or usual source of supply or it can be posted direct to the Manager, Mineral Springs, Buxton, in which case the remittance should be made payable to Buxton Corporation.

Amount of Remittance £   s.   d.

NAME

ADDRESS

Recent correspondence with the present owners of the bottling business, Nestlé gives a picture of the current position of the business:

'...*Tebbs was bought by Canada Dry Rawlings in the 1980s and the water was bottled by their subsidiary, Hooper Struve & Company in their premises in the Hot Charity Baths in George Street. The company was taken over again in 1987 by Perrier (UK) Ltd which was acquired by Nestlé in 1993. When Perrier UK acquired the Buxton Water Company, 600,000 bottles a year were produced. Within two years of taking over Buxton, Perrier moved to a purpose built site next to the Railway Station in Buxton.*

The water is taken from the source to the bottling plant in specially laid stainless steel pipes. In addition to the still and carbonated varieties in sizes ranging from 25cl to 5 litres, the present company, Nestlé Waters UK, offer the water with orange or lemon/lime carbonated flavours in

St Anne's Well in 1996 showing curved feed pipe installed in the 1950s

50cl bottles. EC regulations now define the term 'Mineral Water' very specifically and Buxton water, which satisfies this definition, has been given Natural Mineral Water status.

Buxton is one of the purest natural mineral waters in the world and it continues to lead the market in terms of quality, purity and innovation. Its extensive range of bottle sizes can satisfy all consumer preferences and in the UK this wide range is unmatched. Buxton is the official water for the famous Wimbledon Lawn Tennis Championships, where it refreshes and re-energises the world's greatest tennis players and the 35,000 spectators who are at Wimbledon each day...'[29]

Closure of the Devonshire Royal Hospital and its Baths

Doubts about the viability of the Devonshire Royal Hospital had been voiced in the town from the 1980s. Stockport Health Authority was seeking to rationalise service provision with its intention to close the hospital and provide the services at different centres in and around Buxton, and despite a well run campaign against its closure the hospital finally closed its doors in July 2000.

All the services which had been previously provided at the Devonshire were relocated at the Buxton and Cavendish Hospitals with the exception of rheumatology which was transferred to a purpose built unit at Stepping Hill Hospital in Stockport. The building until this time had been the property of the National Health Service and was now put on the market. The University of Derby showed early interest in acquiring the buildings and mounted a carefully organised campaign to purchase the hospital to use as a town centre campus to replace their college at Harpur Hill.

An announcement was made in January 2001 from the Department of Health that the university had been successful in its bid and ownership of the building changed hands. Conversion of the building took place during 2003 and 2004 at an estimated cost of £8.5 million with the first intake of students in the Spring of 2005. The new campus of the University of Derby College, Buxton will develop as a community university providing a full continuum of learning from basic skills to doctoral research. Significantly it will provide a School of Tourism and Hospitality Management, which aims to become a new international centre of excellence. The 1914 baths suite is is to be refurbished retaining the two hydrotherapy pools as part of the health & beauty training area of the campus.

The Future

Buxton - the Mountain Spa - has re-shaped itself often over time to meet new challenges; changes in fashion, in medicine, in leisure as this history has shown. Always it has sought to exploit its natural attributes, its mineral waters, its scenery, its situation high in the Peak District hills and to capitalise on what it does best - its hospitality to the visitor.

So it is that the two decades leading to the third millennium have seen both a cultural renascence and substantial physical regeneration in Buxton Spa. From the 1979 refurbishment of the Opera House and the birth of a new annual opera and literary festival bringing with it other festivals of Gilbert and Sullivan, jazz, classical, brass and country music, all this supporting a great live music, drama and cultural scene throughout the year. The theatre, standing behind the Opera House, re-opened in 1980 converted to a multi-function hall called the Paxton Suite. After a disastrous fire in 1983 the central hall of the Pavilion was carefully rebuilt in iron and glass style to provide a restaurant and coffee shop.

The Pavilion Gardens can again offer comprehensive facilities for conferences, fairs and a wide range of functions. More recent investment has resulted in a £1.4m refurbishment of the Opera House and entrance to the Pavilion Gardens which has brought both the exterior and interior decoration back to the original design of the architect, Frank Matcham. Between 1997 and 2003 a Heritage Lottery Urban Parks programme of £4.8m has restored the Pavilion Gardens back to the Edward Milner and Robert Rippon Duke original designs of 1871-76.

In 1987/8 a new road to relieve the very congested Spring Gardens was built. This necessitated the removal of the old Midland Railway station, which had closed in 1967, but paved the way for the main commercial street to be pedestrianised in 1997 and for the Spring Gardens Shopping Centre, a modern glass barrel-vaulted design to be built. In 1999 the High Peak Borough Council launched a regeneration scheme to enhance the frontages of retail buildings in Higher Buxton followed by work in 2004 redesigning the Market Place to improve its appearance and to produce a layout which can meet the needs of both traffic and pedestrian in a busy 21st century urban setting.

In the lower town the aspect of John Carr's magnificent Crescent has received much attention and will receive more. The terraced slopes in front of the Crescent, laid out by Jeffry Wyatt in 1818, and modified in the 1840s by Joseph Paxton, were again refurbished in 1993-94 and this work included the replacement of Turner's Memorial in its original position in front of the Hot Baths.

The Georgian Crescent, the Natural Baths and the Victorian Pump Room did not fare well in the

1970s and 80s. In 1970 the Derbyshire County Council bought the east wing of the Crescent which had stood empty for four years after being vacated by the Devonshire Royal Hospital. A comprehensive programme of restoration opened up the building as the County Library and other offices. The Assembly Room, its fibrous plasterwork repainted in authentic colours and the original crystal chandeliers in place, served as the reference library. The west end of the Crescent was occupied by the privately run St Anne's Hotel and the Pump Room housed the Tourist Information Centre.

Progressive deterioration of the St Anne's Hotel due to lack of maintenance and the discovery of structural defects in the library and County Council offices at the eastern end caused the Crescent to be seen as seriously at risk in the early 1990s. A rescue plan by the County and Borough Council with the department of National Heritage, English Heritage and the National Heritage Memorial Fund acquired the St Anne's Hotel and provided a total of £1.5m to effect repairs between 1993-96 to this grade one listed building described by the Georgian Group as the finest Georgian building in the Midlands.

In seeking viable alternative uses for the Crescent, the Buxton Crescent & Spa Project was set up jointly by High Peak Borough Council and Derbyshire County Council. In 2003 they commissioned the Trevor Osbourne Property Group in association with Danubius Hotels, the largest spa hotel group in Europe, to develop the Crescent and spa in a £23m investment. Envisaged in this scheme is:

- An 87-bedroom quality hotel occupying the majority of the Crescent
- A spa in the Natural Baths including development on its roof
- An interpretation centre occupying the basement, ground floor, first floor, second floor (front) and attic of the Crescent
- A re-located tourist information centre alongside the interpretation facility in the ground floor of the Crescent
- A function suite based in the Assembly Rooms of the Crescent which is linked to the hotel
- Eight small retail units in the front ground floor of the Crescent
- A tearoom in the Pump Room
- Environmental enhancements

The spa development will once again bring Buxton Natural mineral water into therapeutic use which, as this history has shown, can be traced back to Roman times and for which there is certainly continuity from Mediaeval times, perhaps spanning 1000 years. The break may hopefully be short for the water was used in the hydrotherapy pools of the Devonshire Royal Hospital until closure in 2000. The new spa and health facility of the university will re-introduce

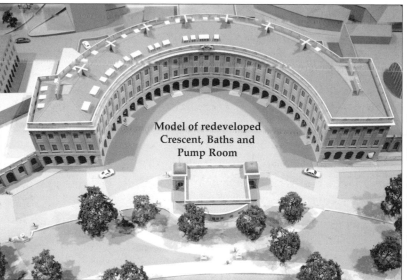

Model of redeveloped Crescent, Baths and Pump Room

By Facade Models of Castle Carey, Somerset

hydropathic techniques and new choices of balneology will be on offer for the visitor and resident.

So Buxton springs forward as spa and university town. Its basis for growth and diversification can be found in its celebrated history, a history full of colour, interest, change and challenge. Out of this history comes a new modern resort with an old name - Buxton Spa.

APPENDIX 2:
Glossary of treatments

Through the 19th century traditional water medicine, influenced by hydropathy and an ever developing range of treatments, progressively gave way to water regimes better described collectively as hydrotherapy. Buxton, in common with its northern rival Harrogate, together with Bath, Droitwich, Leamington and other centres, prescribed a wide range of treatments, which included the use of electricity, for which the general term 'balneology' was used .

Hydrotherapy, with its origins in medical rubbing, runs as a theme through Buxton's maturing health resort. Traditionally doctors had always seen the value of massage or rubbing of the skin during bathing. The shampooers of the 1840s had turned by the end of the century into 'masseurs' and in Buxton, as with other health resorts, electrotherapy ran alongside massage.[1]   In 1904 the Devonshire Hospital had three hon. masseurs and two hon. masseuses as well as a hon. consulting electrical engineer.[2] Electric baths, massage and electro-massage were available, several different forms of massage were used and the town had at least one electrical engineer specialising in electromedical apparatus and several private masseurs and masseuses.[3]

By the end of the century hydrotherapy in health resorts was part of a wider movement of balneology and climatology. Some attempts were made to link water medicine with sanatoria in the treatment of pthisis (tuberculosis - the largest single killer disease of the time) but not many sanatoria used water medicine in the treatment of this disease. The practice was more prevalent in Germany.[4]

The Society of Balneology and Climatology, founded in about 1895 with headquarters and library in London's Cavendish Square, was influential in drawing together and providing professional recognition to all the medical practitioners working in this 'specialist' field. Dr Hyde of Buxton was an early, if not founder member, a Vice-President and Chairman of Council. In 1905 the society had 400 Fellows and, in the same year, Buxton had nine Fellows, all practising in the town, some associated with hydropathic establishments, others hon. medical officers to the Devonshire Hospital. Harrogate, in that year had sixteen Fellows, as did Bath, Droitwich six, Leamington five, Malvern five, Ilkley three and Matlock one, and the pattern was similar for 1906.[5] This suggests that the most successful health resorts were those which had a natural mineral water of some repute and which had developed traditional water treatments supported by a specialist hospital.   Buxton was one such resort.

The glossary which follows describes the treatments mentioned in this account of the history of baths and water medicine in Buxton.

WATER AND OTHER TREATMENTS

Aeration Bath Certain of the small immersion baths at the Hot baths were fitted with aeration apparatus consisting of small holes in the bath walls which could be used to pump air into the bath rather like today's jacuzzi. The recommended length of immersion in an aeration bath was 45 minutes and was usually followed by a hot towel wrap of 20 minutes duration. (See whirlpool bath.)

Aix Douche Massage The patient sat upright in a chair whilst attendants poured streams of hot water over the body and applied massage.

Ascending Douche A perforated seat arrangement in which water was forced under pressure through perforations vertically to the seated patient. Recommended for haemorrhoids, rectal and uterine prolapses, uterine congestions and painful or irregular menstruation. The treatment could also be effected through a jet or spray from a nozzle placed near the level of the floor when it could be used on the soles of the feet. Treatment was offered in a range of water temperatures to suit particular medical conditions.

Bourbon-Lancy Bath Probably replicating the treatment at Bourbon in the south of Burgundy. This is a hot water of 56° to 60°C. which is cooled before being used in a range of treatments. Today the Bourbon-Lancy water treatment is referred to as 'Thermalism' and a technique of 'crenotherapy', based on the absorption of water by the skin is used.

Buxton Douche Massage The patient received this treatment whilst lying in a shallow bath of copper coated with white metal. The water depth was about 7 or 8 inches at a temperature of 93-98°F. (34-36°C) Water was forced onto the body at a temperature of 96-102°F via a douche hose and massage was applied. The treatment lasted 10-15 minutes. Sometimes the douche massage was followed by a douche spray down the spine of the erect patient. The spray was gradually lowered in temperature to as cold as the patient could stand. Following this the patient was wrapped in towels and allowed to rest in the dressing room before dressing.

Buxton Oxygen Bath Within balneology particular attention was paid to the quality of the air and exposure of the patient to fresh air as part of the treatment. The Buxton air was reputed to be particularly invigorating. In an air bath the patient was laid on a bed close to an open window. The assisted air bath added a fan to this arrangement to increase the air flow. This may be seen as a forerunner of the sanatorium style of wards used in the treatment of tuberculosis.

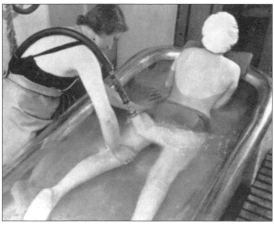
Buxton Masage and Douche

Chalybeate Bath Hot & cold baths using chalybeate or iron-bearing water

Douche The application of a single or multiple column of water against some part of the body. Various types of hose and nozzles were used and treatments varied in relation to temperature, pressure and mass of water used according to the type of complaint being treated. The douche was a widely used form of treatment and many variations existed eg. horizontal jet, vertical jet, fan, broken jet. Special applications of the douche to particular parts of the body or internal organs were separately named eg. dorsal, lumbar, cerebral or gastric douches.

Wet Douche Douche applied when patient is immersed in a bath (sometimes referred to as the undercurrent).

Dry Douche Applied directly to body of patient, usually erect. Descending Douche, what we now know as a shower.

Facial Massage Local massage or 'shampooing' of the face.

Fango Mud Packs A mud made from dark volcanic ash, imported from Italy, and mineral water is applied to the affected part of the body. It is intended to draw the toxins out of the pores and cure arthritic pains

Graduated Cure See Terrain Cure.

Greville Heat Treatment Super heated air was applied to the affected part of the body prior to immersion in a warm bath.

Hubbard Tank Reputed to be the first facility for providing remedial exercises in water, this shallow tank in which the patient was laid supported by slings in a floating position, was developed by American orthopaedic surgeon L.W. Hubbard in 1924. Massage and exercises were given by an attendant. Mr Hubbard was well-known for treating President Franklin D. Roosevelt who was disabled by poliomyelitis.[6]

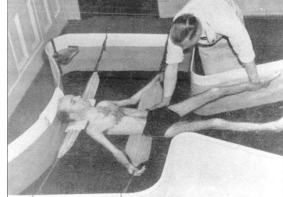
Hubbard Tank

Immersion Bath General term meaning immersion in a single bath. These baths could be taken as 'full', 'three-quarter' or 'half' baths (the latter two being specially indicated in cases where there was cardiac weakness). Most baths were fitted with a crane and seat for lowering the patient. They were administered at varying temperatures. One variant, called the Graduated Bath, commenced at a temperature between 93-98°F and the temperature was decreased in successive baths.

Manicure Cosmetic treatment of the hands & fingernails.

Matlock Bath Bath given at temperature of 68°F (19.8°C), simulating the waters of the Matlock Bath springs.[7]

Immersion Bath.

Medicated Bath A bath prepared with the type of additional medication such as pine, brine, sulphur, carbonic acid. It is possible to conjecture that such baths were replicating the kind of treatment found elsewhere, brine for example, at the Nauheim baths, sulphur in the baths at Bath in Somerset or carbon dioxide at Carlsbad.

Moor or Peat Bath Moor peat was mixed with water and heated by steam injection to a temperature of 90-105°F (32-40°C) to form a paste. The recommended time of immersion in the bath was about twenty minutes but because the hot mixture could induce drowsiness some patients bathed for lesser time. After emerging from the peat the patient was hosed down by the bath assistant and wrapped in hot towels for a further twenty minutes. The treatment was considered effective for skin disorders, rheumatism & sciatica. The peat bath induced profuse sweating and often resulted in a temporary loss of weight. The peat was obtained from the moors surrounding Buxton. A variation of this bath was the peat Sitz bath which immersed the lower torso and thighs in a small bath filled with the peat mixture.

Moor Pack This was designed for those who could not, or preferred not to take the full peat bath. It was prepared to treat individual joints. The patient was laid on a slatted wooden plinth which was covered with a rubber sheet topped with a sheet of calico. The hot peat mixture was packed around the affected joint and the sheet was wrapped around the peat. The pack was left in place for twenty minutes, after which it was removed and the joint was either sponged clean or the patient took an immersion bath.

Mustard Bath As the medicated bath but containing mustard powder. Other materials were added to baths such as: bran, gelatine or nutrients of various kinds.

Mustard Pack Mustard and water mixed to a thick paste and applied to the affected area

Nauheim Bath Effervescent saline bath found naturally in the resort of Bad Nauheim in Germany. The water there is heavily charged with carbonic acid gas and contains, in solution, a large amount of chloride of calcium. The bath was artificially prepared in Buxton and elsewhere by the addition of several chemicals, including carbonate of soda and hydrochloric acid, in particular proportions, to the natural mineral water. It was felt to be very effective in the cure of cardiac and renal cases

Needle Bath or Douche en Circle A series of nearly circular pipes arranged on top of each other which were perforated on their inner surfaces. water was forced through the pipes under pressure, emitting small jets or needles of water on the patient who stood in the middle of the apparatus. The equipment often incorporated the rain or shower douche and the ascending douche.

Pedicure Cosmetic treatment of the feet and toenails.

Plombiere Douche Mineral water enema. First introduced in the French town of Plombiere. Used in cases of colonic disorders.

Russian Bath In this bath the patient lay on a slab in a small room filled with steam. The temperature would range from 115 to 120 °F (46 to 48°C) and the length of the bath 10 to 20 minutes. The treatment might include alternate heat and cold with the patient moving between the steam room and a cold shower. In a Russian Bath the patient would be rubbed by an attendant to promote the early appearance of perspiration. Ailments treated by this method include rheumatic pain, diabetes, dyspepsia and sciatica

Sand Bath Sand was heated to the temperature of 110-120° F (43-48°C) on iron plates. The sand was mixed to obtain an even temperature and applied to the extremities of the patient in a layer 3-4 inches thick and to the abdomen and chest half an inch thick. This encouraged profuse perspiration and formed a crust of sand over the skin which was afterwards washed off by a warm bath. Considered effective in cases of gout, rheumatism and Bright's Disease

Schott Exercises Swedish medical gymnastic exercises adapted by Drs August and Theodore Schott of bad

Nauheim into a programme suitable for the treatment of cardiac disease. These could be used either in conjunction with the Nauheim Bath or alone.

Scottish Douche Two hoses were used alternately, one hot the other cold which were sprayed under pressure onto the standing patient. The hot application was relatively long (1-4 minutes) whilst the cold was short (3 -30 seconds). The application could be applied to a large area of the body or more localised. It was considered good for cases of paralysis, neurasthenia, sciatica and gout.

Shampooing An early term for medical rubbing or massage.

Sitz Bath Small portable bath, made of metal, porcelain or wood of such a form and size that the patient could be seated in it by leaving the feet outside the bath. The lower trunk and upper thighs only were immersed in the Sitz bath and could be taken hot or cold and with or without a douche. Used for conditions of the lower spine and genitalia.

Sitz Bath

Sprays A form of Douche where instead of a single jet the water issues from a perforated head in a considerable number of small streams. Fine water sprays were applied to the throat nose ears & eyes.

Sun Bath In the American version of this treatment the patient was undressed and laid out in front of a south facing window to bathe in the sun's rays for about 15 minutes. In Buxton a 15 minute electric sun heat treatment was followed by a swim in the Natural Bath.

Terrain Cure Buxton was noted for this, so called 'Terrain Cure' or graduated hill climbing. It was also known as the Graduated Cure and the Walking Cure. The exercise was thought to be a valuable part of the treatment for heart weakness and early forms of cardiac degeneration. The terrace slopes in front of the baths at Buxton were considered ideal for this purpose, both doctor and patient could measure the improvement as the patient climbed progressively higher. The Terrain Cure was quite often associated with the Nauheim Bath.

Tivoli Douche From the Italian resort of the same name just north east of Rome. It is a Roman town on the river Aniene which has sulphur baths, so it may be conjectured that this was a douche with an artificial sulphur water.

Turkish Bath An early form of bath dating, at least to Roman times. The Turkish Bath suite in the early 20th century would consist of a steam room followed by a series of progressively hotter dry heat rooms. The rooms were usually communal and various forms of exercise or massage would accompany the stay in each room. A plunge pool, shampoo room and massage were also incorporated. In this description the term 'shampoo' means washing the patient with soap and water and a rough cloth mitten. The cold plunge bath was necessary to close the pores of the skin. After treatment it was usual to relax in a cooling room before leaving.

Vapour Bath Essentially a steam bath. In some cases the patient was enclosed in a cabinet with only the head protruding. Alternatively the half vapour bath enclosed the lower trunk and lower limbs only. Local versions of the apparatus were available to treat individual limbs.

Vichy douche Similar to the Buxton Douche Massage with the patient reclining in a shallow bath but lying on a hot water mattress whilst water was applied to the body and massage given. Also referred to as 'massage sous l'eau'.

Walking Cure See Terrain Cure.

Wax Treatments Introduced into Buxton after the Great War the wax treatment was designed to give relief to patients with rheumatic conditions of the hands & wrists. The affected hand was immersed in a small bath of melted wax for a few seconds. This process was repeated several times, with the patient keeping the fingers perfectly still so as to avoid cracking of the wax. In 1921 'Thermowax' and 'Flexol' Baths were offered as new treatments for stiff and painful

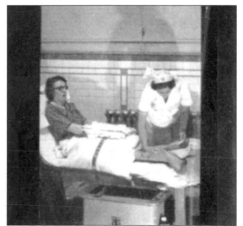
Paraffin Wax Therapy.

joints. The 'Thermowax' treatment was the outcome of experiments in military hospitals during the Great War and the 'Flexol' Bath was developed at the Devonshire Hospital and only available at Buxton.

Whirlpool Bath Small bath for one person with swirling and bubbling water. Equivalent to today's Jacuzzi.

ELECTRICAL TREATMENTS

Artificial Sunlight - Exposure of the body to ultraviolet rays, equivalent to present day solarium.

Bergonie System Developed by Jean Bergonie, a French physician, this involved rhythmical and graduated methods of muscular exercises by galvanic and faradic stimulation of various muscle groups. It was particularly recommended for obesity and might be used in conjunction with the radiant heat bath.

D'Arsonval High Frequency Treatment D'Arsonval of Paris was a respected specialist in hydrotherapy working in the late 19th century. He conducted a number of experiments and designed equipment including a portable calorimeter for assessing fever in a patient. His high frequency treatment involved the use of electrical current and was a form of Diathermy.

Diathermy Application of high frequency electric currents to produce heat in the deep tissues of the body. Also described in terms of High Frequency Currents (10 & 20 Mins) and Static Currents (10 & 20 Mins). Used for the relief of pain, to improve circulation and increase the range of joint movement.

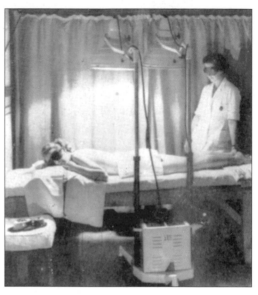

Artificial Sunlight.

Dowsing Radiant Light & Heat Treatment This was prescribed for the treatment of stiff and painful joints and a range of additional complaints including rheumatism, gout, sciatica and lumbago. It consisted of a metal bed with heated panels and rows of light bulbs surrounding the patient.

Electric Light Bath A wardrobe-like piece of apparatus which was lined with rows of electric light bulbs on its inner surfaces. The patient stood in the middle of this arrangement and in certain cases a spray douche was applied. Various other forms of apparatus, using rows of light bulbs, were devised to treat parts of the body, for example, the spine, trunk, legs, feet or hands.

Electro 4 Cell Schnee bath An apparatus which could be used for the treatment of the whole body or for local applications. It consisted of a specially designed seat with feet and arm baths attached. Current, via a switchboard, could be directed through the body in various configurations. It was considered useful for certain local applications, for example in cases of hemiplegia one arm and one leg could be treated together or for frostbite the two legs or two hands could be immersed.

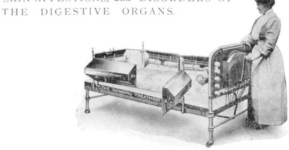

The DOWSING
Radiant Heat and Light Treatment.

The DOWSING system of TREATMENT is prescribed by the Medical Profession for the treatment of RHEUMATISM, GOUT, RHEUMATOID ARTHRITIS, LUMBAGO, SCIATICA, SPRAIN, STIFF & PAINFUL JOINTS, CHRONIC BRIGHT'S DISEASE, CHRONIC ARTICULAR RHEUMATISM, STIFFNESS, FRACTURED LIMBS, SKIN AFFECTIONS, and DISORDERS OF THE DIGESTIVE ORGANS.

DOWSING BED APPARATUS FOR WHOLE BODY.

Installed at The Thermal Mineral Baths, Buxton, and at all the important spas, hydros, hospitals, nursing homes, etc.

Electro-Water Bath, General With the patient immersed in a porcelain, glazed earthenware or wooden bath at a temperature of 92-98° F (33-36°C), electricity was applied to the body via a stationary head plate and sliding

DR. SCHNEE'S FOUR-CELL BATH.

Schnee Four Cell Bath.

metallic electrodes on each side. The strength of the current which could be either direct or alternating, was increased to such a level that a distinct tingling sensation could be detected by the patient. Recommended for the treatment of insomnia, it is not difficult to imagine that this treatment had the potential to be a permanent solution for that problem! This bath was frequently used in hospitals to treat children suffering from infantile paralysis.

Electro-Water Bath, Local The use of a vessel in which one part of the body, for example, arm of leg, was immersed in water. Usually one electrode was placed in the bath and the other on the patient's body thus the current ran through the patient and could be accurately measured.

Faradisation The use of interrupted or alternating current to produce muscle contractions to correspond with the make and break of the current. It delivered nerve and muscle stimulation in a form of electrical massage and was found useful for, neurasthenia and hysteria, general debility, nervous dyspepsia, anaemia and for conditions where improved circulation was needed.

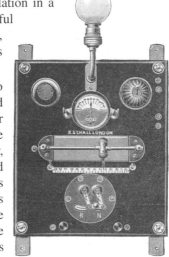

Galvanic apparatus

Galvanism or Galvanic Treatment The application of direct or constant current to the skin using a medical battery and different types of electrodes. Galvanism was used both therapeutically and for diagnostic purposes. It could be applied in a fixed manner to one part of the body or moved up and down or on and off the affected part to produce friction to the skin. It was recommended for Insomnia, Neurasthenia, General debility, Hysteria, Rickets and Anaemia and a range of other conditions such as Chillblains and Frostbite, spasmodic conditions such as writer's cramp and to effect electrolic changes for removal of hairs or warts. Central Galvanism involved the treatment of the nervous system for insomnia and neurasthenia using a large flat metal electrode and sponge applied across the forehead, down each side of the neck and along the length of the spine.[7] The medical term 'Neurasthenia' was popular at the turn of the century. It was used to describe a broad range of conditions, including general nervousness, depression and chronic fatigue, and could be said to be the male equivalent of the diagnosis 'Hysteria' in females, which usually also implied a physical disability that was believed to be imaginary - such a diagnosis for a man of course being inappropriate in the 19th century.[8]

Ionisation or Ionic Medication or Cataphoresis Static electricity was applied to the body in much the same way as in galvanism but the active electrodes were padded and soaked in weak solutions of various chemicals. The theory behind the process was that current passing through the chemicals created ions (charged atoms) of that particular salt. The treatment was based on the assumption that the current forced the curative ions through the skin and into the body. Thus chlorine ions from a solution of sodium chloride were used to treat inflammatory fibrous tissue, lithium was used for gout and rheumatic diseases, zinc and copper for antiseptic and stimulating effect, cocaine and morphine ions for neuralgias and quinine ions for some cases of neuralgia. It was described by local doctors as the method of passing remedies through the unbroken skin by means of electricity. [9]

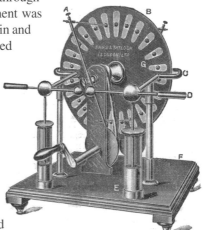

Static Electricity in Medicine A method of giving shocks to the patient by means of a machine for generating static electricity. One such machine, sometimes seen in school physics laboratories, was the Wimshurst static Machine. The patient is insulated by being placed on a glass platform and positive or negative current is applied. It was used for functional nerve diseases such as hysteria, neurasthenia, insomnia, nervous headaches and obscure neuralgias.

Wimshurst machine

REFERENCES AND NOTES

Prologue

1. Martin, A. MD. *Historical Sketch of Balneology* Medical Life, Vol. 34. no. 5. May 1927. Carbon dioxide dissolved in water produces a weak acid known as Carbonic acid.
2. Hembry, Phylis, *The English Spa 1560-1815 A Social History* London 1990 Ch. two; See also Introductory Note no. 6.
3. *Ibid.* pp. 42-43
4. Granville, A.B. *The Spas of England 2. The Midlands & South*, London 1841 (Reprinted Bath 1971)
5. Short, T. MD *The Natural, Experimental and Medicinal History of the Mineral Waters of Derbyshire, Lincolnshire and Yorkshire*, London 1734
6. Parker, Brenda J. *Brenda Hunt's The West Hallam Heritage* , Ilkeston 1987 p.93
7. Platts, T. L. *A Spa in Sheffield - The History of Birley Spa* Sheffield 1976
8. Hembry *op. cit.* p. 285

Chapter 1

1. Garton, D. 'Buxton' Current Archaeology, No. 103, 1987
2. Hart C.R. North Derbyshire Archaeological Survey, Sheffield City Museums, 1984
3. Jewitt, A. *The History of Buxton*, Buxton 1811 pp.13-16.
4. Leach, J. *The Book of Buxton*, Buckingham, 1987, pp. 28; Internet website www.roman-britain.org/places/aquae_arnemetiae. htm
5. Wroe, P. 'Roman Roads in the Peak District' Derbyshire Archaeological Journal [DAJ] Vol. C11, 1982
6. Tristram E., 'Roman Buxton ' DAJ. Vol XXXV111, 1916; The Roman Britain website at note 4. above suggests the distance to Anavio as eleven thousand paces (11 Roman miles) and Edward Tristram does offer some doubt over whether the number of Roman miles should be 10 or 12.
7. Turner, W. FSA *The Reliquary* May1903; Salt, WH. Reliquary and Archaeologist, April1900
8. Makepeace G. 'The Roman-British Settlement at Staden near Buxton: 1987-88 and 1989-90 Excavations and Final Report.' DAJ. Vol. 115, 1995
9. Bramwell D. et al 'Excavations at Poole's Cavern', DAJ. 1983; also Branigan K. & Bayley J. DAJ. Vol. CIX 1989
10. Leach, J. *op. cit.*, 1987, pp. 27   11. Tristram E., op. cit. pp. 86/7
12. Walker J., 'Buxton: The Natural Baths' , Trent & Peak Archaeological Trust, 1994
13. Leigh, C. *The Natural History of Lancashire, Cheshire and the Peak in Derbyshire*, Oxford 1700; The Romans developed a fine hard lime cement which used pozzolana, a reddish volcanic dust, whose properties allow it to set in damp conditions. Sera, R. Roman Architecture, nd. London p.73.
14. Short T., MD. *The Natural, Experimental and Medical History of the Mineral Waters of Derbyshire, Lincolnshire and Yorkshire*, London 1734.
15. Leach J. 'Buxton Well Chapel' occasional Paper no. 2, Buxton Archaeological & Natural HistorySociety, Bulletin no. 2 Autumn 1986
16. Floyer Sir J., *An Enquiry into the Right Uses and Abuses of the Hot and Cold Temperate Baths in England*, 1697
17. Denman J. MD. *Observations on Buxton Water*, editions of 1793 and 1801
18. Pearson, G., *Observations and Experiments for Investigating the Chymical History of the Tepid Springs of Buxton*, London 1784.
19. Hart, C.R. op. cit. 1984
20. Johnson, J.S. *Chesters Roman Fort*, English Heritage, London, 2001, pp. 11-18; Ward, A.M. & Brown, M.H. *Melandra Roman Fort an Illustrated Guide*, Glossop.
21. Page, W. FSA. *The Victorian History of the County of Derby*, Vol 1, 1905, pp. 225; www.roman-britain.org/places/aquae-arnemetiae.htm The VHC of Derby thinks the evidence for a shrine is thin and that Rooke's plans of site buildings are practically useless. The Roman Britain website is more assured in its description of the temple.
22. Axon, E. Historical Notes on Buxton, its inhabitants and visitors, Paper no. XIX, c. 1944
23. Kennedy C. W. *The Earliest English Poetry,* Oxford University Press, 1943
24. Martin, G.H. Keeper of Public Records, 'Domesday Book' address given at Westminster Abbey 29 April 1986, unpublished Mss.
25. Makepeace G. op. cit. 1995.
26. Cameron K. *The Place Names of Derbyshire* Part I, English Place Name Society, 1993
27. Axon, E. op. cit. paper no. 5. November 1937
28. Jones J. *The Benefit of the auncient Bathes of Buckstones, which cureth most greevous sicknesses, never before published.* London, 1572
29. Axon E. op. cit., Paper no.3. 1936
30. *Ibid.* 31. *Ibid* 32. Axon E. op. cit. paper no.4. November 1936 33. *Ibid.* 34. Axon E. op. cit. paper no. 5. November 1937
35. Axon, E. op. cit. paper 2. October/November 1934. Sir Thomas Wentworth (1593-1641) was the first Earl of Stafford (cr. 1640) a politician and statesman of strong principles. A Royalist and close adviser to Charles I, he was executed by Parliament on Tower Hill in May 1641. *Dictionary of National Biography*, Oxford 1948.
36. Jones J., op. cit. 1572.
37. Batho G.R. *A Calender of the Shrewsbury and Talbot Papers* Vol II, HMSO 1971
38. *Ibid.* Vol. F Folio 157; Guy, J. *My Heart is my Own, the Life of Mary Queen of Scots*, London 2004, pp. 442-48 & 518, offers a valuable account of the background to her visits to Buxton Spa.
39. Hembry, Phyllis, *The English Spa 1560-1815*, The Athlone Press London, 1990.
40. Axon, E. op. cit. paper 2
41. Batho G.R. *op. cit.* Vol. G Folio37
42. Fraser Antonia, *Mary Queen of Scots*, Weidenfeld & Nicolson,1969
43. Portland papers, Vol. l Folio 105, Longleat House, Warminster
44. Langham, M. 'Things Written in the Glasse Windowes at Buxstons', Derbyshire Miscellany, Vol 15 Pt 1. Spring 1998
45. Camden, W., *Brittania*, MDCVII, Translated and enlarged by Gough, R. London 1789, Derbyshire [Coritani] p. 303
46. Axon, E. op. cit. papers no 2.& no.19. Lady Arabella (Arbeila) Stuart (1575-1615) was niece to Henry Stuart, Lord Darnley, the second husband of Mary Queen of Scots. Next in line to the throne after James I. Bingham, Caroline, *James Vl of Scotland*, London 1979, pp. 157; DNB Concise 1948 under 'Arabella Stuart'; See also Gristwood, Sarah, *Arbella - England's Lost Queen*, London 2004, pp. 321-23.

Chapter 2.

1. Camden, W., *Brittania*, MDCVII, Translated and enlarged by Gough, R. London 1789, Derbyshire [Coritani] p. 303. 1st edition 1586 but 6th edition of 1607 greatly enlarged.
2. Drayton M., *A Chorographical Description of this Renowned Isle of Great Britain*, 1622
3. Axon E. op. cit. paper no.1. nd.   4. Axon E. op. cit. paper no. 6. March 1938
5. Hobbes T. *De Mirabilibus Pecci* London, c.1636
6. Cotton, C. *The Wonders of the Peake*, 1681, H. Brome of the Gun, St Paul's Churchyard
7. Thornes R. & Leach J., 'Buxton Hall', Derbyshire Archaeological Journal Vol. CXIV 1994
8. Short, T. MD., *The Natural, Experimental and Medical History of the Mineral Waters of, Derbyshire, Lincolnshire and Yorkshire*, London, 1734, pp. 23-53
9. Morris C. *The Journeys of Celia Feinnes*. 1949. London The Cresset Press
10. Browne, E. A Journey through the Midland Counties in September 1662. Reprinted in *Reliquary* Vol.XI. 1870/71; Edward Browne was an eighteen year old medical student when he did the tour but he went on to become President of the College of Physicians. Axon, E. op. cit paper no. 2. Oct/Nov. 1934.
11. Floyer Sir J., *An Enquiry into the Right Uses and Abuses of the Hot and Cold Temperate Baths in England*, 1697

12. Leigh, C. *The Natural History of Lancashire, Cheshire and the Peak of Derbyshire*, 1700

13. Hall. l. *Georgian Buxton,* Derbyshire Museum Service. 1984. Also Barker Deeds, BAR P666, Sheffield City Archive

14. Short T., MD. op. cit London 1734. pp. 23-53

15. The Bodleian Library, Oxford, Shelfmark Ms. Top. gen.e. 61, fol. 14r

16. Axon, E. op. cit. paper XIX, November/December 1944

17. Axon, E. op. cit. paper no. 1. nd.; See also Furbank P.N. & Owens W.R. *Daniel Defoe, A Tour* London 1991 pp. 241-42, 246, 249.

18. An Act for repairing and widening the road from Sherbrook-Hill near Buxton and Chappel in the Frith, in the County of Derbys, to Manchester in the County of Lancashire, George II Regis 9 Oct 1722, London, John Baskett, Printer to the King 1724.

19. Roberts, A.F. *Turnpike Roads around Buxton,* Buxton 1992, pp. 17 & 89; Leach J *The Book of Buxton*. 1987 Buckingham, p. 112

20. Thornes R. & Leach J., op. cit. 1994

21. Short, T. *op. cit.* pp. 25-53   22. *Ibid* pp. pp. 23-53   23. *Ibid* pp. pp. 23-53

24. Hunter A . *A Treatise on the nature and virtues of Buxton Waters,* 1768; Pearson. G. MD *Observations and experiments for investigating the chymical history of the tepid springs of Buxton,* London 1784. Vol 1.

25. Hall. l. *op. cit.* 1984

26. Buxton Estate Accounts, 'Building accounts of John Carr', C41 9 vols. Devonshire Collections, Chatsworth.

27. Denman Jos. MD. *Observations on Buxton Water*, editions of 1793 and 1801

28. Buxton Estate Accounts, 'T' Series Collection of Joseph Fletcher 1790 - 1797 and Joseph Gould 1798 -1804, Devonshire Collections, Chatsworth

29. Axon E. FSA Historical notes on Buxton, its inhabitants and visitors. Paper 1.

30. Anon. England Displayed. 1769

31. Axon E. FSA. op. cit. Paper XV111, Music & Dancing

32. Wells C. *The Buxton Stage*. Disley 1998

33. Stukeley W. *Itineraries Curium*. London 1725

34. Byng J. *The Torrington Diaries.* 1790

35. Leach J. *op. cit.* 1987; Langham, M. *Buxton - A People's History,* Lancaster 2001, pp. 38

36. Faujas Saint-Fond B. *Travels in England, Scotland and the Hebrides*. London 1799.

37. Allen, B.. Dr. *Natural History of Mineral Waters* 1711; Short, T. *op. cit.* pp. 25-53

38. Denman J. MD. *op. cit.*

39. Jewitt A. *op. cit.* 1811.

40. Pearson. G. MD. *op. cit.* 1784

41. Transcribed in E. Bradbury, *Wardley's Gossiping Guides to the Peak*, No. 2. Castleton etc., Buxton, 1892, pp.26

42. Axon E. FSA. op. cit. Paper XV11, Early Local Government, October & November 1943.

43. *Ibid*

44. Bradbury E., *Pictures of the Peak*, London, 1891

Chapter 3

1. White J. Jun., 'Plan for Improvements at Buxton; 1803 revised 1806'. Map 2042, Devonshire Collections, Chatsworth

2. Denman J. MD. *op. cit.* 1793 and 1801

3. Buxton Estate Accounts 1806 - 1820, Devonshire Collections, Chatsworth

4. Heacock P. letter 1st January 1810 and earlier correspondence, Letterbooks of P. Heacock, Devonshire Collections, Chatsworth

5. Jewitt A. op.cit. 1811

6. Scudamore, Sir C. MD, *A Chemical and Medical Report of the Properties of the Mineral Waters of Buxton, Matlock, Cheltenham [et al]* London, 1820; *The Analysis and Medical Properties of the Tepid Springs of Buxton*, 3rd edn. London 1839

7. Carstairs, T., MD, *Bathing and Buxton Waters* , editions of 1847 and 1853

8. 'Old Plan of Baths Approaches and the Square as existing prior to the alterations about 1851' Buxton Museum Collection

9. Bott, W. A , *Description of Buxton and Adjacent Country etc.* Manchester 1795, passim.

10. *Hutchinson's Tour through the High Peak of Derbyshire*, Macclesfield 1809, pp. 136-7

11. Jewitt A. *op. cit.* 1811, pp. 136-149. The Charitable Institution is the Buxton Bath Charity, see Langham, M.J. & Wells, C. *A History of the Devonshire Royal Hospital,* Leek, 2003; The new walks she refers to are the Hall Gardens and Serpentine which were modified the following year in a similar manner to the suggestions of her brother; and re-modelled frequently throughout the 19th century; The Ebbing and Flowing Well was near Barmoor Clough; The Derbyshire diamond is actually fluorospar, a translucent form of gypsum; W Bray's *Sketch of a Tour into Derbyshire and Yorkshire* was first published in 1778.

12. Plan of baths water management, c. 1820, High Peak Borough Council, Buxton.

13. Adam W. *Gem of the Peak*, editions of 1845 and 1851; Buxton Advertiser 18 october 1902.

14. Buxton Estate Accounts 1820-1833, Devonshire Collections, Chatsworth. See also Scudamore, Sir C., MD, The Analysis and Medical Account of the Tepid Springs of Buxton, 2nd ed. 1833 which describes the female Charity Bath.

15. Robertson, W.H. *Buxton and its Waters*, London and Buxton, 1838, p.77.

16. Langham M.J. *Buxton - A People's History,* Lancaster 2001, ch. 1. passim; Axon, E. op. cit paper XVIII, May/June 1944.

17. Orme, D. *The New Buxton Guide,* Macclesfield 1823, pp.33-34. Bright's jewellers in the Square moved to the Crescent in about 1835.

18. *Bewick to Dovaston: Letters 1824-1828*, Natali & Maurice publ 1968

19. Whitbread, Helena (Ed.) *No Priest But Love - The Journals of Anne Lister from 1824-1826*, Otley 1992. p.111-118

20. Orme, D. *The New Buxton Guide*, 1823 and The Buxton Guide, 1842; Robertson, W.H. Buxton and its Waters, 1838

21. Page T.J. *The Buxton Bather's Handbook, Brief Observations on the Buxton Waters*, 1843

22. Langham M.J. & Wells C. *The Architect of Victorian Buxton*, Derbyshire County Library Service, 1996

23. Robertson, W.H. *op. cit.* 1838, pp. 32-34

24. *Ibid* pp. 104-05

25. Bowden, Annie, 'The Making of the Devonshire Royal Hospital', Buxton, Salford School of Occupational Therapy, unpublished thesis 1991; Scudamore, Sir C. MD, *op. cit.* 1839; Berkeley, G. Revd, *Siris - A Chain of Philosophical Reflections and Inquiries Concerning the Virtues of Tar Water*, London, 1744

26. Page T.J. *op. cit.* 1843

27. Bednall, A.W. [Ed] 'Taking the Waters in Buxton - 1836', Unpublished Mss, Macclesfield 1985.

28. *Chambers Beauties of Buxton*, Buxton 1841, J.B. Chambers publ.

29. Granville, A.B. *Spas of England and Principal Sea Bathing Places*, 1841. (Reprinted 1971, Bath) Vol. 2.

30. *Builder Magazine,* August 20. 1853

31. Langham M.J. *op. cit.* 2001, pp.41-2

32. *Illustrated London News*, August 26. 1854; Robertson W.H., A Handbook to the Peak of Derbyshire and to the use of the Buxton Mineral Waters, Buxton 1854; Devonshire Buxton Accounts, 1852 - 60, Devonshire Collections, Chatsworth

33. Pilkington J., *A View of the Present State of Derbyshire* 1789.

34. Denman J. MD. *op. cit.* 1801, pp. 49-50

35. Orme, D. *The Buxton Guide*, 1842 and Pigot & Co.'s Directory of Derbyshire 1835

36. *Freebody's Directory of Towns of Derbyshire* 1852

37. Auctioneer's catalogue 7.11.1860, Langham & Wells Collection, Buxton

38. Croston J., *On Foot Through the Peak*, 9th edition 1889; Ward Lock, *Illustrated Guides to Buxton and the Peak District* etc. 1891, 1894; Robinson W.H. (sic) *Popular Guide to Buxton* etc.1896; Baddeley M.J.B. *The Peak District of Derbyshire*, editions of 1891, 1894, 1912

39. Ward Lock & Co., *Buxton, The Peak, Dovedale*, London, 1918-19 and 1927-28; We are indebted to Oliver and Marjorie Gomersal for their personal recollections on the use of this bath; Buxton Advertiser July 1946.

40. Pearson, J. A. *Reports of Cases Treated at the Buxton Bath Charity and Devonshire Hospital between May 1st and October 31st 1860*, Liverpool 1861

41. Robertson W. H., *Handbook to the Peak of Derbyshire* Buxton, Editions of 1861, 1864, 1866, 1868, 1872, 1886

42. Langham, M.J. & Wells, C. *The Architect of Victorian Buxton*, Matlock, 1996, ch. 6; History of the Devonshire Royal Hospital at Buxton, Leek, 2003.

43. Langham M.J. *op. Cit.* 2001, pp. 115-120

44. Croston, J. *op. cit.*, 1889, pp. 316-17

45. Bradbury, E., *Pilgrimages in the Peak, Buxton*, 1879, pp. 14-15. The schottish is a ballroom dance fashionable in the nineteenth century and the composer Dan[iel Eyers] Godfrey (1868-1939) became the conductor of the seaside orchestra at Bournemouth which he raised over time to a full symphony orchestra.

46. Langham M.J. & Wells C. *Buxton Waters*, Derby, 1986; *A History of the Devonshire Royal Hospital at Buxton*, Leek, 2003, pp.84.

47. Buxton Medical Society, *Buxton its Climate, Baths and Waters*, nd. (c. 1905); Buxton its History, Waters, Climate, Scenery etc. 1905

48. Robertson W.H. *A Guide to the use of the Buxton Waters*, Buxton, 1896

49. Buxton Medical Society, *Buxton its Climate, Baths and Waters*, nd. (c. 1905) pp. 16-20.

Chapter 4.

1. *Buxton Advertiser* editions of: 2 December 1900; 9 March; 11 May; 1 June; 22 June 1901; Buxton Library, Local Studies

2. Buxton Baths Capital Expenditure Accounts, Langham & Wells papers, Buxton

3. Leach John, *The Book of Buxton*. Buckingham, 1987.

4. Hacker, Art, *Buxton thro' other Glasses*, Derby, 1905.

5. *Buxton Advertiser* editions: 24 April 1903; 23 Jan 1904; 9 April; 21 May; 31 Dec 1904; Langham M. J. op. cit 2001, ch. 4. appx. 2. pp. 237; See note 2.

6. *Buxton Advertiser*, 30 July 1912.

7. Armstrong Wm. & Harbum J.E., *Buxton, Its Waters, Baths and Accessory Methods of Treatment*, Bristol, 1911.

8. Hyde, S. MD., *Buxton, Its Baths and Climate*, Manchester. 1895; See also appendix 1.

9. Wells, C. *The Buxton Stage*, Disley 1998

10. Buxton Official Handbook Bureau of Information, Buxton, 1921; Mortimer, M., *The Spirit of Cavendish Golf Club - 1899-1999*, Droitwich, 2000.

11. 'Natural Baths, Buxton, Proposed Reconstruction Ground Plan 1915 and 1921', Engineer & Surveyor, Buxton Borough Council.

12. *Buxton Advertiser* 17 May 1924; Souvenir Programme Buxton Corporation, 1924, Langham Papers, Buxton.

13. Bradshaw, Ray, 'Working Life of Buxton 1947-63', Private research papers.

14. Bradshaw, Ray, Conversation with the Duchess of Devonshire for 'Working Life of Buxton 1947 - 63', Private research papers.

15. M Langham & C Wells. 'William Radford Bryden FRIBA. A Short Biography.' Buxton Archaeological & Natural History Society Bulletin No 28 Autumn 1999; *A History of the Devonshire Royal Hospital at Buxton*,. Leek, 2003, pp. 83-84

16. 'Devonshire Hospital, Plan of proposed new baths.1913' . D4508/31/2. Derbyshire Records office, Matlock.

17. *Buxton Advertiser* 26 April 1935; Buxton Official Guide, 1935.

18. Papers on 'Collaboration with the Empire Rheumatism Council, 1937', D4508/47/1, Derbyshire Record office, Matlock; 'All Through the Years' issued by the Devonshire Royal Hospital c. 1937, The Langham Papers, Buxton.

19. 'A Scheme for the Provision of Hospital and specialist services at the Rheumatism Centre, Buxton. April 1947' The Langham Papers Buxton

20. 'Mineral Water Baths, St Anne's Well, Wash Baths and Bottling Stores', undated plan, Langham & Wells collection, Buxton.

21. Bradshaw, R. *op. cit.*

22. Langham, M. & Wells, C. *Buxton Waters*, Derby, 1986

23. 'Buxton Thermal Baths 1952-63' 3 Plans, D1317., Derbyshire Record Office, Matlock.

24. Bradshaw, R. op. cit

25. *Ibid*; Bentley, M., Langham M.J. & Wells C., *Buxton from the Board Collection*, Stroud, 1999, p. 91.

26. Buxton Advertiser , editions of 1986, passim.

27. Axon, E. op. cit. Paper no. 1. nd.

28. Buxton Officiai Handbooks 1909 and 1914, Buxton Corporation.

29. Correspondence with Daphne Barratt of Infoplan International Public Relations, 4 February 2004

Also a series of Buxton handbooks issued annually by the Buxton U.D.C. and Borough Council 1900-1974 from the Buxton Library, Local Studies section and authors' library

Appendices

1. R. Rolls, 'From Balneology to Physiotherapy: the development of physical treatment at Bath' in R. Rolls and Jean and J. Guy (eds.), 'A Pox on the Provinces' Proceedings of the 12th Congress of the British Society for the History of Medicine, Bath 1990. pp. 111-118

2. Report of the Devonshire Hospital and Buxton Bath Charity, 1904. Derbyshire Records office, D4508/10/5.

3. S. Hyde, *op. cit.* 1898 pp. 94-103 & 43; *Kelly's Directory of Derbyshire* 1904; Professional recognition for medical rubbers came through the Society of Trained Masseurs founded in 1894. By 1900 membership was 250. The society then became the Incorporated Society of Trained Masseurs with professional and legal status. Examination entry included the theory of Galvanism and Faradism, the use of electric baths and radiant heat and light. Nicola R.Y. Clemence, 'Physiotherapy - A Hundred Years of Medical Rubbing?' Norfolk & Norwich Institute for Medical Education Journal, Vol. 10, Autumn 1993. pp. 31-36; E.M. Magill, Notes on Galvanism and Faradism, London 1919, 2nd ed.

4. M. Worboys, 'Urban Advantage-Tuberculosis 1885-1925' Unpublished paper, Sheffield, 6 Oct 1997; C.J. Whitby, 'Notes on the Sanatorium Treatment of Pthisis and its Present Limitations', Journal of Balneology and Climatology, Vol. 9. Pt. 1, 1905.

5. op. cit. , Vol. 9, pt. 4, Oct 1905; Vol. 10, pt. 4, oct 1906.   In 1905 Buxton had twenty doctors in total.

6. Crebbin-Bailey, Jane, Harcup J. & Harrington J., *The Spa Book*, London 2004.

7. Pentecost A. *The Thermal Springs of Matlock Bath*, nd. The Spa Handbook Series.

8. Magill, E.M. *Notes on Galvanism and Faradism*, London, 1919 2nd edn., pp. 50, 73-74.

9. Armstrong, W. & Harburn, J.E., *Buxton, Its Waters, Baths and Accessory Methods of Treatment*, Bristol, 1911.

INDEX